10. 00

Service and the Ministry of Reconciliation: A Missiological History of Mennonite Central Committee

by Alain Epp Weaver

Bethel College
North Newton, Kansas
2020

Cover photos: MCC worker Jeanne Zimmerly Jantzi with Congolese women, 1993. (MCC photo/Dan Jantzi) MCC workers Ali Mia (left) and George Klassen in Bangladesh, 1979. (MCC photo/Charmayne Brubaker)

Wedel Series logo by Angela Goering Miller

ISBN 1-889239-13-5

Cornelius H. Wedel Historical Series

1 Rodney J. Sawatsky, *Authority and Identity: The Dynamics of the General Conference Mennonite Church*, 1987

2 James C. Juhnke, *Dialogue with a Heritage: Cornelius H. Wedel and the Beginnings of Bethel College*, 1987

3 W. R. Estep, *Religious Liberty: Heritage and Responsibility*, 1988

4 John B. Toews, ed., *Letters from Susan: A Woman's View of the Russian Mennonite Experience (1928-1941)*, 1988

5 Louise Hawkley and James C. Juhnke, eds., *Nonviolent America: History through the Eyes of Peace*, 1993, 2004

6 Al Reimer, *Mennonite Literary Voices: Past and Present*, 1993

7 Abraham Friesen, *History and Renewal in the Anabaptist/Mennonite Tradition*, 1994

8 James C. Juhnke, *Creative Crusader: Edmund G. Kaufman and Mennonite Community*, 1994

9 Alain Epp Weaver, ed., *Mennonite Theology in Face of Modernity: Essays in Honor of Gordon D. Kaufman*, 1996

10 Sjouke Voolstra, *Menno Simons: His Image and Message*, 1996

11 Robert S. Kreider, *Looking Back into the Future*, 1998

12 Royden Loewen, *Hidden Worlds: Revisiting the Mennonite Migrants of the 1870s*, 2001

13 Jean Janzen, *Elements of Faithful Writing*, 2004

14 H. G. Mannhardt, *The Danzig Mennonite Church*, 2007

15 Jaime Prieto, *Mennonites in Latin America: Historical Sketches*, 2008

16 Jaime Prieto, *Menonitas en América Latina: Bosquejos Históricos*, 2008

17 Wilhelm Mannhardt, *The Military Service Exemption of the Mennonites of Provincial Prussia*, 2013

18 Mark Jantzen, Mary S. Sprunger, and John D. Thiesen, eds., *European Mennonites and the Challenge of Modernity over Five Centuries: Contributors, Detractors, and Adapters*, 2015

19 James C. Juhnke, *A People of Two Kingdoms II: Stories of Kansas Mennonites in Politics*, 2016

20 Walter Sawatsky, *Going Global with God as Mennonites for the 21st Century*, 2017

21 Alain Epp Weaver, *Service and the Ministry of Reconciliation: A Missiological History of Mennonite Central Committee*, 2020

Series editor: vols. 1-4, David A. Haury
vols. 5-21, John D. Thiesen

For my parents, Anthony and Dianne Epp, models of Christian service

Contents

Series Preface   ix

Acknowledgements   xi

Introduction   xiii

1 The Ministry of Reconciliation   1

2 Constructing Christian Service: The Landscapes of MCC   14

3 Listening and Waiting: Shifting Understandings of Service
      in MCC   43

4 First to the Household of Faith? MCC, Humanitarianism,
      and the Church   66

5 Presence, Connection, Solidarity, Measurement:
      Missiologies in Tension in MCC   97

Index   125

Series Preface

The Cornelius H. Wedel Historical Series was initiated by the Mennonite Library and Archives at Bethel College as part of the college centennial celebration in 1987. Cornelius H. Wedel, the first president of Bethel College from the beginning of classes in 1893 until his death in 1910, was an early scholar of Mennonite studies. His four-volume survey of Mennonite history, published from 1900 to 1904, helped to rescue Anabaptism and Mennonitism from their marginal and denigrated portrayal in standard works of church history. Wedel saw Anabaptism and Mennonitism as part of a tradition of biblical faithfulness going back to the early church.

Wedel also believed in the cultivation of the intellect in all fields of knowledge. The Wedel Series furthers this goal by publishing research in Mennonite studies with a special emphasis on works with a connection to Bethel College, such as campus lecture series and projects based on the holdings of the Mennonite Library and Archives.

Of the twenty volumes published in the series prior to this time, thirteen have originated in campus lecture series or symposia, five arose out of library or archival holdings at Bethel College, and two had both ties. One volume has been reprinted since its original publication. Topics in the series have included Mennonite identity, biography and autobiography, Bethel College history, nonviolent interpretations of United States history, Menno Simons, Mennonite literature, and theology.

The volume you have before you, based on the 2019 Menno Simons lectures at Bethel College, offers missiological reflections on one hundred years of Mennonite Central Committee's relief, development, and peace work.

John D. Thiesen
Series Editor

Acknowledgements

Many thanks to all at Bethel College involved in inviting me to present the 67th annual Menno Simons lectures at Bethel in October 2019 and in hosting me so warmly, including Kip Wedel, John Thiesen, Mark Jantzen, Rachel Epp Buller, and Melanie Zuercher. Presenting the Menno Simons lectures at my alma mater was an honor and a privilege. Frank Peachey and Lori Wise from the MCC U.S. records department proved able guides through MCC's archives, while Fred Yocum and Brenda Burkholder of the MCC U.S. communications department helped identify striking photos that capture key moments from MCC's one hundred years. I owe an immense debt of gratitude to Sonia Weaver, who encouraged me throughout the research and writing process. Sonia's inquisitive curiosity, fearless readiness to immerse herself in unfamiliar contexts, and her passionate commitment to justice prodded us to embark on our first MCC assignment, an assignment that has decisively shaped my professional and intellectual life and that impressed on me that Christian service is ultimately less about doing and more about patient listening, readiness to question one's preconceptions, humility not just to give but also to receive, and sharing life with others over cups of coffee, tea, and simple meals. Finally, a word of appreciation and gratitude for my parents, Anthony (d. 2011) and Dianne Epp. I first learned about MCC from their stories of teaching through MCC in Congo and then from volunteering with them at a fair trade store in Lincoln, Nebraska, that sold items from MCC's SELFHELP Crafts venture. My father has joined the great cloud of witnesses who inspire and urge us on to lives of Christ-centered service, while my mother pieces MCC comforters that are shipped around the world and bakes pies and zwiebach for the Kansas Mennonite Relief Sale that supports MCC. To the extent that I understand anything about the meaning of Christian service, it is in large part thanks to them, and for that I am eternally grateful.

Alain Epp Weaver
Lancaster, Pennsylvania
August 2020

Introduction

Initially developed as a temporary, *ad hoc* initiative in 1920 of multiple Mennonite churches and organizations in the United States and Canada to respond to the famine faced by Mennonites in what was then part of southern Russia and is now Ukraine, Mennonite Central Committee (MCC) has grown over the ensuing decades into a worldwide ministry of Anabaptist churches carrying out relief, development, and peacebuilding programs in the name of Christ in over fifty countries. Arguably no other institution has done as much as MCC to shape and construct global understandings of what it meant and means to be Mennonite in the twentieth and twenty-first centuries, apart from perhaps Mennonite World Conference.[1]

This book, developed from the 2019 Menno Simons lectures delivered at Bethel College in North Newton, Kansas, reflects on the evolving and sometimes competing missiologies that have emerged from within and shaped MCC's practice of Christian service over the course of a century. The ensuing chapters dissect and analyze the shifts, tensions, and persistent themes in how MCC has understood its mission, paying attention to how such service unfolded within and was shaped by specific landscapes.

For most of this book's readers, MCC is probably already something of a known quantity. Perhaps you have worked for MCC—maybe as a Pax volunteer in the 1950s in post-World War II Europe, or with the Teachers Abroad Program in the 1960s in a post-colonial African country, or at an MCC office in the United States or Canada. Perhaps you have hosted a young adult from Africa, Asia, or Latin America serving in Canada or the U.S. for a year as part of MCC's International Volunteer Exchange Program. Maybe you have packed school kits and relief buckets or stitched and knotted comforters at an MCC material resources center or have volunteered when MCC's mobile meat canner rolls into town. You may volunteer or shop (or both!) at an MCC

---

[1] Throughout this book, when I refer to MCC as a "Mennonite," "Anabaptist," "inter-Mennonite," or "inter-Anabaptist" agency, I do so as a shorthand way to name the wide variety of churches that have supported and continue to support MCC and have representation on MCC's governance boards, including Beachy Amish, Mennonite Brethren, Mennonite Church USA and Mennonite Church Canada (and their predecessors), Brethren in Christ, Conservative Mennonite, Old Order Amish, and more.

thrift shop, or maybe you donate quilts and bake pies for an MCC relief sale. Perhaps children in your congregation collect pennies, nickels, dimes, and quarters for MCC through My Coins Count, and maybe you give money regularly to MCC. If you are among the set of readers who have in some way participated in MCC's service in the name of Christ, I hope you will find in this book new ways of thinking about how your part of the MCC story fits within broader directions and tensions across MCC's century-long history.

For a smaller group of readers, this book may be the first you have heard of MCC. If that is the case, my hope is that you nevertheless find questions addressed in these chapters that prod you to think about the nature of Christian service. While the book's chapters examine different aspects of MCC's history and present practice, each asks questions relevant to contexts beyond Mennonites and MCC. Taken together, these chapters reflect on the meaning of Christian service through the case study of MCC, which has "service in the name of Christ" as one of its mottos. By examining shifts and tensions within MCC's relief, development, and peacebuilding work across one hundred years, the book poses broader questions about who Christian service is for, questions such as: What communities does Christian service form? Who is understood to be serving whom? Where does Christian service happen? How is Christian service shaped by contexts of colonialism, racism, and gendered hierarchies? How does Christian service relate to broader humanitarian discourses?

The book's first chapter addresses these questions in a sermonic and overtly theological fashion, describing MCC as engaged in a "ministry of reconciliation" that ultimately is not about a whirlwind of *doing* or one-way giving from those who have to those who have not, but instead about the discovery of fellowship and sharing with one another through expanding inter-Anabaptist, ecumenical, and other networks in which all come before God with empty hands, ready to receive and share God's good gifts.

The remaining chapters adopt a more historical stance, analyzing how MCC's missiology—in particular, its under-standing of Christian service—has been a site of contestation throughout the organization's history. MCC's service in the name of Christ has been ever evolving and mutating, often hotly debated, and always under construction. Chapter 2 develops this broader framework of analyzing MCC's missiology as perpetually under construction and as a site of contestation. It then fleshes out this framework by examining how MCC's missiology and self-understanding have been constructed within specific geographies, including expanding inter-Anabaptist and ecumenical landscapes and geographies of poverty, hunger, war, racism, and colonial legacies.

In chapter 3, attention turns to the varied meanings of Christian service within MCC and how those meanings have shifted over time. How have passions for Christian service mirrored or conflicted with the patriotic call to serve one's country? Is the language of service inherently unidirectional and thus inextricably bound up with potentially racist, paternalistic, and neo-colonial imaginations of "us" going "out" to help "them"? Or can service be conceptualized not as unidirectional giving but instead as mutual sharing? The changing valences of the word "service" over the course of a century within MCC will spur reflection on such questions.

Chapter 4 explores the Christian roots of humanitarianism as a universalizing ideology of providing assistance without consideration of particular characteristics such as race and religion and tensions between that universalizing vision and the specific call to help one's family, immediate neighbors, and fellow Christians. The apostle Paul's admonition to the church in Galatia to "work for the good of all, and especially for those of the household of faith" (Galatians 6:10, NRSV), which served as a frequent touchstone for MCC in its first decades, embodies this tension—a call to universal love, charity, and good deeds, but with the particular starting point of the church. As a humanitarian relief organization like MCC seeks to manage limited resources faithfully, negotiating this tension represents an enduring challenge. What distinctive roles do partnerships with local congregations and denominational agencies play for international Christian organizations in carrying out relief, development, and peacebuilding ministries?

The final chapter looks at how MCC's missiology in its second half-century has been shaped by critiques of development discourses that emerged in the 1970s and 1980s and the ways that development agencies sought to respond and adapt to those critiques. Failures of educational, agricultural, health, and other interventions in the global South by external actors such as United Nations agencies, donor governments, and international NGOs like MCC led to sustained critique within the development world of past efforts, with some seeking to reform development practice and others wondering if the development enterprise should be jettisoned altogether. Following an assessment of how such debates played out within MCC in the seventies and eighties, the chapter proceeds to examine keywords that have shaped MCC missiologies over the past four or five decades, examining how terms like *presence, connect, solidarity*, and *measure* have operated and sometimes clashed within MCC's internal discourse.

Born in the wake of global crises such as the devastation of the First World War and the so-called "Spanish Flu" pandemic of 1918, MCC has continued over the ensuing decades to serve in the name of Christ amidst multiple crises. As I write this introduction, the COVID-19 pandemic shapes and disrupts the global contexts where MCC operates, even as the climate crisis upends the lives of the world's most vulnerable communities and as wars in places like Syria and the Democratic Republic of the Congo leave millions upon millions displaced from their homes. MCC's missiology has been tested and molded by such crises over a century.

If operation in the midst of crisis runs as a through line across MCC's history, so can one also discern a recurrent theme of collaboration among diverse Anabaptist groups in Canada and the U.S. to respond boldly to these crises, from cooperation to feed Mennonites on the brink of starvation in southern Russia in the early 1920s to joint action through MCC to accompany vulnerable communities around the world whose lives have been made even more precarious due to COVID-19. Such collaborative construction of a shared inter-Anabaptist commitment to Christian service has not been free of conflict: indeed, contestation over the meaning of Christian service has surfaced repeatedly across MCC's history. Yet even within such conflict, unity amidst diversity has been formed time and again through the movement of God's Spirit.[2] As MCC enters its second century, may the Spirit continue to move to create ever new and expanding global networks and bonds of fellowship through collaborative efforts to reach out to neighbors and enemies in ministries of relief, development, and peace.

---

[2] One thread woven throughout this book is how MCC, in addition to implementing its relief, development, and peacebuilding programs, has repeatedly functioned as an ecumenical driver, constructing context-specific unity in collaborative action amidst diversity of belief and practice, with this collaborative action in turn contributing to evolving networks of Mennonite identity and continuously shifting understandings of Christian service. Recognition of this role played by MCC is explicitly named in multiple essays in *Unity Amidst Diversity: Mennonite Central Committee at 75* (Akron, PA: MCC, 1996) and Alain Epp Weaver, ed., *A Table of Sharing: Mennonite Central Committee and the Expanding Networks of Mennonite Identity* (Telford, PA: Cascadia, 2011).

Chapter 1: The Ministry of Reconciliation

Adapted from a sermon preached at Bethel College Mennonite Church on October 27, 2019
   2 Corinthians 5:14-21; Luke 24:13-35

Every year, Mennonite Central Committee (MCC) chooses a passage from Scripture to focus its public communication about its relief, development, and peacebuilding work carried out in the name of Christ. As we drew closer to MCC's centennial year in 2020, I wondered what scriptural verses MCC's communications team would highlight to commemorate the MCC century. Two contenders came readily to mind. One possibility, I surmised, might be Jesus' parable of the good Samaritan (Luke 10:25-37), with its story of neighbor love manifested as humanitarian action that does not discriminate, but rather extends care to all, regardless of religious conviction, a care that upends narrow conceptions of who is our neighbor and who belongs to our household of concern.

A second possibility, I speculated, could be Jesus' account to his disciples in the gospel of Matthew of the day of judgment, in which the nations of the world will come before the Son of Man in his glory to be separated out as sheep and goats, with the sheep, the ones who inherit God's Kingdom, being those who gave food to the hungry, offered water to the thirsty, and welcomed strangers (Matthew 25:31-46). After all, this story had inspired the title of a 1988 MCC history by Robert Kreider and Rachel Waltner Goossen.[1] The imagery of extending a cup of water to the thirsty has become a potent symbol for the humanitarian relief efforts that have run as a consistent thread across MCC's ten decades, from its beginnings in responding to famine among Mennonites and others in southern Russia in the early 1920s, to hundreds of relief aid shipments sent to devastated European communities after the Second World War, to canned meat sent to hospitals and orphanages in the Democratic People's Republic of Korea (North Korea) and comforters and relief buckets distributed through Syrian churches in the present day. Both passages, I reasoned, captured

---

[1] Robert Kreider and Rachel Waltner Goossen, *Hungry, Thirsty, a Stranger: The MCC Experience* (Scottdale, PA: Herald Press, 1988).

something essential about MCC's history and present identity and would underscore the scriptural grounding of MCC's humanitarian efforts.

My predictions missed the mark, however, with my MCC communications colleagues choosing neither of the passages I had thought they might, but rather a passage that talks first about our reconciliation to God in Christ, and then about the ministry of reconciliation entrusted to the church, a portion of Paul's second letter to the church at Corinth. In 2 Corinthians 5:14-21, Paul, in the NRSV translation, reminds his readers that "the love of Christ urges us on," with Jesus' followers living "no longer for themselves, but for him who died and was raised for them." In light of Jesus' resurrection, Paul explains, "we regard no one from a human point of view," but rather see a "new creation" whenever anyone is in Christ, with everything old having passed away and everything becoming new. "All this is from God," Paul continues, "who has reconciled us to himself through Christ, and has given us the ministry of reconciliation," entrusting "the message of reconciliation to us" and making us "ambassadors for Christ," with God "making his appeal through us." By choosing this Pauline passage as its focus Scripture for its centennial year, MCC has identified its work as a "ministry of reconciliation."

I confess to some initial surprise upon the announcement of MCC's centennial Scripture passage. While I do not pretend to have a comprehensive knowledge of MCC's substantial archives, I did spend a fair amount of time reading over MCC board minutes, staff reports, worker correspondence, and other files in preparation for the 2019 Menno Simons lectures at Bethel about MCC and its missiology, and this section of Paul's second letter to the Corinthians does not figure prominently within MCC's history. A Scripture passage with more concrete examples of practical *doing* seemed warranted, I felt (at least initially). If not the Good Samaritan parable or Jesus' urging his disciples to care for the "least of these," then why not Jesus' call to his disciples to embody nonresistant love by going a second mile in response to those who would compel them to go one mile (Matthew 5:38-42)? That section of Jesus' Sermon on the Mount has a rich history within MCC, cited by workers in MCC-administered

Civilian Public Service (CPS) camps during World War II, in which Mennonites and others performed tasks of "national importance" as state-sanctioned alternatives to military service (fig. 1) and by those in MCC's Pax program through which young Mennonites carried out alternative service in post-World War II Europe and beyond. While some within these programs undertook this service grudgingly, many MCC workers wrote of their desire to go beyond serving as so-called "conscripted Christians," to instead become "willing second milers," seizing the opportunity to transform their compulsory service into an opportunity to demonstrate the practical power and effectiveness of nonresistant love through tangible acts of service.[2]

Fig. 1: Glenn Smith, Forest Service Squad Leader, adjusts the parachute of smoke jumper Harry Mishler at CPS Unit No. 103 in Huson, Missoula County, Montana. Year unknown. The unit operated from 1943 to 1946. (MCC photo)

But again, neither Jesus' commandment to embody nonresistant love by going the second mile in service nor another Scripture passage describing concrete acts of service was chosen as MCC's centennial focus Scripture. Instead, we have Paul's exhortation to Jesus' followers that, in being reconciled to Christ, they have been given a ministry of reconciliation. Drawing from this passage from Second Corinthians, how might we understand MCC's history and its present work as a "ministry of reconciliation?" What do we gain by framing MCC's work as participating in the ministry of reconciliation given to the church?

---

[2] For a fuller discussion of Pax and CPS workers seeking to "go the second mile," see chapter 3 below.

Fig. 2: Ronald Mathies, a participant in MCC's Teachers Abroad Program (TAP), talks in 1972 with students at Henry Henderson Institute in Malawi. (MCC photo)

One way to tell MCC's history is as a furious churn of *doing*. MCC has sent out young people to serve—as orderlies in mental hospitals during World War II as part of the MCC-run CPS program in the United States, as construction workers with MCC's Pax program tasked with building a highway across Paraguay's Chaco region in the fifties, as educators in the sixties and seventies in post-colonial contexts in countries across Africa through the Teachers Abroad Program (fig. 2), as community development workers across Latin America, Africa, and Asia in the 1980s, and more.

MCC has also channeled volunteer energies in Mennonite, Mennonite Brethren, Brethren in Christ, Beachy Amish, Old Order Amish, and other Anabaptist communities in the U.S. and Canada. Church communities mobilize to can meat, pack school kits and relief buckets, and raise money by organizing relief sales and operating thrift shops.

Finally, MCC has served as an incubator and catalyst for the development of a wide variety of initiatives that later spun off from MCC. An incomplete list of such institutions includes: Mennonite Disaster Service, which marshals post-disaster recovery and reconstruction efforts after hurricanes, floods, and other disasters in Canada and the United States[3]; mental health facilities in the U.S. established in the aftermath of World War II by Mennonites moved by the testimonies of former Civilian Public Service workers appalled at the state of care in the United States for people with mental illness[4]; the SELFHELP Crafts fair trade venture that started out of the trunk of Edna Ruth Byler's car and later became Ten Thousand Villages; and the ecumenical

Fig. 3: In 2015, Mohammed Suleman, mayor of Shakha Piska in the Kurdistan Region of Iraq, stands in front of the spillway of a dam constructed by MCC partner, REACH, with support from MCC and the Canadian Foodgrains Bank (CFGB). (MCC photo/Matthew Sawatzky)

[3] For a popular account of Mennonite Disaster Service's history, see Lowell Detweiler, *The Hammer Rings Hope: Photos and Stories from Fifty Years of Mennonite Disaster Service* (Scottdale, PA: Herald Press, 2000). Brenda D. Phillips assesses recent MDS efforts (its responses to Hurricanes Katrina and Ike in 2005 and 2008, respectively) in *Mennonite Disaster Service: Building a Therapeutic Community after the Gulf Coast Storms* (Plymouth, UK: Lexington Books, 2014).

[4] For overviews and analyses of the Mennonite mental health movement that emerged from Civilian Public Service experiences, see Robert Kreider, *The Responsibility of the Church to the Mentally Ill* (Scottdale, PA: Gospel Herald Press, 1945); Titus W. Bender, "The Mennonite Mental Health Movement and the Wider Society in the United States," *Journal of Mennonite Studies* 29 (2011): 45-60; Abraham M. Nussbaum, "The Mennonite Mental Health Movement: Discipleship, Nonresistance, and the Communal Care of People with Mental Illness in Late-20th Century America," *Journal of Nervous and Mental Disease* 200, no. 12 (December 2012): 1088-1095; Alex Sareyan, *The Turning Point: How Persons of Conscience Brought about Major Change in the Care of America's Mentally Ill* (Scottdale: Herald Press, 1994); and Steven J. Taylor, *Acts of Conscience: World War II, Mental Institutions, and Religious Objectors* (Syracuse, NY: Syracuse University Press, 2009).

partnership of Canadian Foodgrains Bank, in which Canadian farmers dedicate profits from some of their fields to support food aid and food security initiatives (fig. 3).[5]

MCC has undeniably involved a non-stop flurry of doing, a myriad of ways in which Anabaptists and others from Canada, the U.S., and beyond have carried out acts of service. In a decades-old slogan, MCC has underscored that this doing, this service, is "In the Name of Christ." Yet this profession that MCC service is done "In the Name of Christ" has not prevented some Mennonites from repeatedly worrying, from at least the 1950s onwards, that MCC service risked becoming decoupled from witness, a concern often expressed as anxiety over the separation of "word" from "deed."

One of the earliest articulations of this anxiety surfaced in a 1957 "MCC Relief Study Committee" of the Eastern Mennonite Board of Missions and Charities in Salunga, Pennsylvania. Eastern Board members were especially anxious that an "over-emphasis" on what they termed "purely social service" might, in their words, "have a definite bearing on the motivations and convictions of young people who serve in MCC and leave them with the habit of social concern and possibly a lessened compulsion for evangelistic witness."[6] The Eastern Board report prompted MCC to convene a broad consultation in 1958 with representation from Anabaptist denominations and mission agencies about the relationship between service and mission.[7]

Worries about MCC relief, development, and peacebuilding work becoming unmoored from Christian mission have regularly resurfaced on an almost cyclical basis across the past

---

[5] For a fuller discussion of MCC as an incubator of initiatives that have gone on to become independent organizations, see Paul Heidebrecht, "MCC As Incubator of New Approaches in Relief, Development, and Peacebuilding," *Intersections: MCC Theory and Practice Quarterly* 8, no. 2 (Spring 2020): 24-25.

[6] Eastern Mennonite Board of Missions and Charities, "MCC Relief Study Committee," 84, in folder Docuware/Binational (BN) Minutes & Meeting Packets 1920 to 2012, Mennonite Central Committee Executive Committee Meeting Minutes, #248, September 14, 1957, Exhibit 17, MCC U.S. archives, Akron, Pennsylvania.

[7] "Minutes of the Study Meeting on the Relationship of MCC Relief and Service Programs and Mennonite Missions," held at Mennonite Home Mission, Chicago, IL, January 24, 1958, in folder Docuware/Binational (BN) Minutes & Meeting Packets 1920 to 2012, MCC U.S. archives, Akron, Pennsylvania.

six decades, with such anxieties in turn spurring MCC to articulate anew how it understood its work as Christian mission. Writing in 1961, MCC leader Peter Dyck acknowledged worries about the decoupling of word and deed, while not conceding their validity. Dyck observed that some critics of MCC portrayed MCC as having bridges to countries around the world, but with nothing to carry across those bridges (in supposed contrast to Mennonite mission agencies, which had a message to carry but lacked the bridges of MCC's global connection). Dyck strenuously objected to this characterization of MCC as lacking a proactive message and as bereft of an understanding of itself as engaged in witness. MCC service, done in the name of Christ, Dyck countered, flowed from and testified to God's love made flesh in Jesus.[8] A few years later, on the occasion of MCC's fiftieth anniversary in 1970, Dyck advanced a more fully developed "theology of service" for MCC, with service embodying a witness to and pointing beyond itself towards the deeper truth of humanity's reconciliation to God through Christ. Authentic Christian service, in Dyck's words, was "eschatological hope made visible." MCC service is thus authentic Christian service when it both embodies and gestures towards this coming hope, standing as an enfleshed testimony within a fallen world to the ultimate victory of God's redemptive love, a testimony to God's reign of love and justice that even now breaks into normalized structures of injustice, shattering our complacency, upending oppressive hierarchies, and offering tentative foretastes of a humanity and creation reconciled to God.[9]

After my initial surprise at the choice of Paul's reminder to the church in Corinth of their reconciliation to God through Christ as MCC's focal Scripture passage for its centennial year, I came to appreciate this decision as the latest in a decades-long effort by MCC to continuously renew and rearticulate the rootedness

---

[8] Peter J. Dyck, "Proposed New Patterns of Cooperation," January 1961, in Cornelius J. Dyck, ed., *Responding to Worldwide Needs: In Europe, the Middle East, Africa, Asia . . . The Mennonite Central Committee Story*, Vol. 2: Documents (Scottdale, PA: Herald Press, 1980), 51.

[9] Peter J. Dyck, "A Theology of Service," *Mennonite Quarterly Review* 44, no. 3 (July 1970): 262-280.

of its relief, development, and peacebuilding work within God's reconciling mission in the world. Over the course of my 2019 Menno Simons lectures at Bethel College (the ensuing four chapters of this book), I examined MCC's one hundred-year history of service as an ongoing and never-settled process of discerning what it means to serve as ambassadors of Christ entrusted with the ministry of reconciliation. This history of the MCC century through a missiological lens traces shifts and probes tensions in the meaning of Christian service within MCC over the past hundred years. MCC's history is undoubtedly in part a glorious kaleidoscope of doing, a creative production of new projects and initiatives. But Paul's letter to the Corinthian church serves as a reminder that this hum of activity has as its foundation, and should continually point us back towards, our reconciliation to God through Christ. In 2003, long-time MCC worker in Central America, Susan Classen, who had accompanied communities in El Salvador and Guatemala during years of military repression and revolution, insisted that "If MCC is to continue into the future, we will need to root ourselves in a spirituality of service." Service, Classen continued, is not ultimately about following a rule or a command to feed the hungry or extend a cup of cold water, but is rather a response of praise and thanksgiving to God's work in our lives.[10]

Luke's account of two disciples who unknowingly encounter and walk with Jesus on the road to Emmaus, two disciples who only recognize Jesus as they break bread together, illuminates that the Christian life is not ultimately about doing, but about connection and fellowship, not about the time and gifts we condescend to give to others out of our strength and our wealth, but rather a mutual sharing of gifts with one another as we come before God in our common need. As I discuss further in chapter 3 below, Christian service always bears with it the danger of spiritual harm and degradation, a unilateral movement from those who mistakenly view themselves as self-sufficient towards those whom the ones extending service falsely define in terms of

---

[10] Susan Classen, *A Spirituality of Service: Freely Give, Freely Receive*, MCC Occasional Paper No. 29 (Akron, PA: January 2003), 4, 7. See also Ted Koontz, "Commitments and Complications in Doing Good," *Mennonite Quarterly Review* 70, no. 1 (January 1996): 59-80.

their need. The Emmaus story prods us to think about service in a different way, reminding us that, like the bewildered disciples hesitant and unsure about whether or not to trust news of Jesus' resurrection after the crushing horror and despair of the crucifixion, we encounter Jesus not in our bounty nor in our self-sufficiency, but in our need. Christian service certainly involves doing, lots of doing—but fundamentally Christian service is about connection to and fellowship with others, discovering ourselves before God in our common need.

In her study of a variety of Finnish humanitarians—from staff of the Finnish Red Cross to the people (mostly women and mostly older) who knit and crochet "aid bunnies," stuffed animals distributed by the Finnish Red Cross along with its humanitarian aid packages—anthropologist Liisa Malkki analyzes humanitarian action in terms of the diverse needs of humanitarian actors. Malkki's ethnographic fieldwork challenges limited understandings of need, shifting focus from those who hunger and thirst to those who seek to help. The humanitarian actors she interviews reflect on where this "need to help" comes from. Some connect it to a need, or a pressing desire, for adventure, for breaking out of numbing routine, and for self-transcendence. Others describe the need to help as a need for connection and belonging. "Seeing the urge to help as proceeding simply from compassion assumes that compassion is yours to give," Malkki reflects. It assumes "that you are working from a position of relative strength." Yet, she continues, the Finns making aid bunnies "were giving less out of strength than out of a kind of fragility," a need to forge and discover connection with others (fig. 4).[11]

What would it look like to tell MCC's century-long story not in terms of the service that Mennonites have extended outwards to others in Canada and the U.S. and in scores of countries around the world, but instead by asking what has driven this Mennonite need to help for the past hundred years? I would suggest that this need to help stems in part from a longing for deeper connection, fellowship, and even communion. MCC's founding

---

[11] Liisa Malkki, *The Need to Help: The Domestic Arts of International Humanitarianism* (Durham, NC: Duke University Press, 2015), 164.

Fig. 4: Lois Sauder, Phyl Leaman, Carol Zook, and Keren Arevalo tie comforter knots at the MCC East Coast Material Resources Center in Ephrata, Pennsylvania, in January 2020. (MCC photo/Jim Wiegner)

involved the collaboration of Mennonite groups that harbored intense distrust of one another, with differences in doctrine and practice both symptoms and drivers of their division. The uniting of these churches in the common cause of service, first in Hillsboro, Kansas, in mid-July 1920, and then again later that month, as a broader group of Mennonite church representatives, in Elkhart, Indiana, was a tentative affair. In some ways, that tentativeness has persisted throughout MCC's history, with questions raised time and again, up until the present, about whether these diverse churches were and are prepared to collaborate in Christian service through this MCC mechanism. Yet through these often tentative collaborations—through thrift shops, relief sales, comforter blitzes, meat canning, and service in CPS camps, Pax crews, and MCC program units—members of churches have also come to recognize their connection, their common need before God and their need for one another. Yes, this fellowship may be tentative—a fleeting eschatological foretaste of our communion with God and one another that breaks into our world of divisions and fractures. By God's grace, however, it is a fellowship that has been renewed time and again. Furthermore, this fellowship has expanded as Mennonites have forged ecumenical and interreligious bonds through MCC service—with Quakers and Brethren in establishing Civilian Public Service; with Mennonites not only from France, Germany, Switzerland, and the Netherlands, but also India, Congo, Indonesia, and Colombia; with Baptists and Pentecostals in Ukraine, Coptic Orthodox in Egypt (fig. 5), and Catholics in El Salvador; and with Muslims and Jews in Palestine-Israel, Hindus in India, and Buddhists in Laos. In breaking bread with these ecumenical and interreligious partners around the world, Mennonites have learned to see themselves not just as doers and not just as givers, but as people in need of connection, fellowship, and reconciliation.

Over the decades, MCC has been privileged to accompany churches and communities around the world as they not only serve their neighbors, but discover an expanded circle of care and common need through that service. In February 2018, I was at the Syrian Orthodox church in the old city of Hama in central Syria. MCC has accompanied the church in Hama as it provides regular food assistance to hundreds of internally displaced families who have come to Hama from across Syria.[12] These

Fig. 5: In 2014, Magda Samir (left), a literacy student at St. Mark and St. George Coptic Orthodox Church in Der Elbarsha, Egypt, takes a pop quiz from Tolba Gad Ekladios, an administrator of the MCC-supported project. (MCC photo)

[12] For a longer reflection on the witness of the Syrian church amidst the country's civil war, see Alain Epp Weaver, "The Mother of the Belt and the Church's Witness in Syria: An Ascension Sermon," *Anabaptist Witness* 6, no. 1 (April 2019): 15-24.

families were among the more than 11 million people uprooted from their homes since the start of the civil war that has ravaged Syria, with at least five million ending up as refugees outside the country and another six million displaced within Syria. The families had fled to Hama from Raqqa, where the so-called Islamic State had set up its caliphate, from Idlib, under siege at the time by Syrian army forces, and from scores of other towns and villages, seeking safety and refuge. On the day I visited Hama, these families had gathered for a shared meal at the church. Offering this meal, with MCC support, was one way that the church in Hama has been faithful to Christ's call to feed the hungry, give drink to the thirsty, and welcome the stranger. As we sat down to eat, however, I was struck even more by how, in serving the meal, the church faithfully carried out the ministry of reconciliation entrusted to it by God. The church in Hama has not been unscathed by the war. Its members have lost loved ones—family and friends have been killed, others kidnapped, many most likely never to be seen again. The displaced who had fled to Hama, meanwhile, included Muslims and Christians, they included Syrians whose families had fought on different sides of a complex, multi-sided war, people who might have good reasons for not wanting to eat together. Gathered in their common need, these Syrians served one another rice, meat, bread, and yoghurt, sharing with one another about their families, struggles, and hopes. This sharing of food in Hama was a foretaste, for me at least, of the reconciliation of all in Christ: in serving the meal and in welcoming refugees, the church in Hama has served as a faithful ambassador of Christ, bearing the ministry of reconciliation given to it by God and in so doing offering a vision of that great feast to which God is gathering all peoples (fig. 6).

To be sure, this meal was a fleeting vision, like all glimpses of God's reign in our fallen world. This meal organized by the church in Hama for refugees from across Syria did not end the war: the powers of sin and death continue to tear the country apart. Yet in organizing the meal, the church gave an embodied witness to what Syria might yet one day be, and to the coming future in which all will stand in fellowship before God in our shared need. Similarly, MCC service in the name of Christ, with

Fig. 6: A meal in February 2018 at the Syrian Orthodox Church in Hama, Syria, with internally displaced families who received monthly food packages distributed by the church with support from MCC. (MCC photo/Emily Loewen)

its buzz of volunteer energies and almost unending succession of new initiatives, also does not decisively end hunger, eradicate poverty, or bring warfare to an end. Yet, through MCC's relief, development, and peacebuilding initiatives, MCC volunteers and workers have acted and continue to act as ambassadors of Christ, pointing beyond themselves to the reconciliation of all to God. I conclude with a prayer for MCC's second century: As we go out in service, our hands busy canning meat, piecing and knotting comforters, and packing school kits and relief buckets, may God also empty our hands, revealing to us our need, and opening our eyes to the coming communion God's reconciling work has already brought about, both close to home and around the world. Amen.

Chapter 2: Constructing Christian Service: The Landscapes of MCC

At the start of the 2019 Menno Simons lectures at Bethel College, I opened with a land acknowledgment, a practice that has become widespread across Canada and increasingly in the United States. Multiple MCC offices in Canada and the U.S. now have signs that commemorate the Indigenous histories of the land on which they are located, thanking Indigenous peoples for their care for the land, remembering their histories of dispossession, and acknowledging ongoing Indigenous presence. These land acknowledgments are also stated orally at the beginning of significant meetings. At the start of the Menno Simons lectures, I asked the gathered audience to join me in a recognition that the lectures were being held on the traditional land of Native peoples, noting that central Kansas is the traditional homeland of several Indigenous nations, including the Wichita, Kaw, and Osage. We recalled that in 1830 the Indian Removal Act resulted in many other Indigenous peoples coming to Kansas, some through treaty and some through forcible removal. The U.S. government then uprooted most Indigenous nations from Kansas in the late nineteenth century, sending them to Oklahoma. We concluded with a moment of silence to lament the suffering of Indigenous nations who once had thriving villages and livelihoods in Kansas, to honor with gratitude their care for the land, and to remember the ongoing Indigenous presence in the land.

Constructing Christian Service

The act of land recognition links to an undercurrent running throughout this chapter, namely, the importance of landscapes to the construction of individual and corporate identity.[1] In this chapter, I narrate MCC's history through an examination of some of the landscapes on which MCC's project of "service in

---

[1] My understandings of space, place, and landscape have been shaped by multiple theorists, including Doreen Massey, *Space, Place, Gender* (Minneapolis: University of Minnesota Press, 1994); Henri Lefebvre, *The Production of Space*, trans. Donald Nicholson-Smith (Oxford: Blackwell, 1992); Michel de Certeau, *The Practice of Everyday Life*, trans. Steven F. Rendall (Berkeley: University of California Press, 1984); and Philip Sheldrake, *Spaces for the Sacred: Place, Memory, and Identity* (Baltimore: Johns Hopkins Press, 2001).

the name of Christ" has unfolded and of the imagined geographies the MCC experience has generated. This historical account makes no pretense at comprehensiveness. Like many other attempts to narrate MCC's history over the past seventy years, this chapter will inevitably have something of a fragmentary character, offering and analyzing select snapshots of the MCC experience.[2] To the extent that this chapter has a unifying theme, it is the claim that what MCC's service in the name of Christ means has never been static, has often been contested, and has always been under construction.

Words such as *construction,* *contestation,* and *imagined* underscore that what it means to "serve in the name of Christ"

---

[2] John Unruh's *In the Name of Christ: A History of the Mennonite Central Committee* (Scottdale, PA: Herald Press, 1952), written when MCC was three decades old, could reasonably strive to achieve a comprehensive account of the organization up to that point. Over the ensuing decades, several publishing projects presented overviews of the breadth of the MCC experience, but in a more episodic fashion. Multiple articles in *Mennonite Quarterly Review* 44, no. 3 (July 1970) examined MCC's relief work, theology of service, peace witness, material aid program, and staffing trends for the occasion of MCC's fiftieth anniversary. The five volumes of *The Mennonite Central Committee Story* (Scottdale, PA: Herald Press, 1980-1988) included books of excerpts from primary documents and a book of stories from individual MCC workers and culminated in Robert Kreider and Rachel Waltner Goossen's *Hungry, Thirsty, a Stranger* (Scottdale, PA: Herald Press, 1988) which had the flow of a chronological history but which by necessity, given the geographic breadth of MCC work and the proliferating diversity of MCC programs, eschewed any pretense of comprehensiveness and focused chapters on representative programs and initiatives. Edited volumes for MCC's silver anniversary (*Unity Amidst Diversity: Mennonite Central Committee at 75* [Akron, PA: MCC, 1996]) and ninetieth anniversary (Alain Epp Weaver, ed., *A Table of Sharing: Mennonite Central Committee and the Expanding Networks of Mennonite Identity* [Telford, PA: Cascadia, 2011]) similarly presented focused investigations of select parts of MCC program. Rather than telling one MCC master story, these narrations of MCC's history reveal an ever-proliferating number of MCC stories. Lucille Marr discusses the importance of "story" in MCC's self-narration in "The History of Mennonite Central Committee: Developing a Genre," *Journal of Mennonite Studies* 23 (2005): 47-58.

Article- and book-length histories of specific MCC programs or parts of the MCC network abound, most notably Esther Epp-Tiessen, *Mennonite Central Committee in Canada: A History* (Winnipeg, MB: CMU Press, 2013) and Lucille Marr, *The Transforming Power of a Century: Mennonite Central Committee and Its Evolution in Ontario* (Kitchener, ON: Pandora Press, 2003), as do memoirs by individual MCC workers.

has never in MCC's experience been something fixed and given, but has always been a matter of negotiation and sometimes conflict. The anthropologist Philip Fountain, who conducted ethnographic work studying the operations of MCC Indonesia in the years following the December 2004 tsunami in the Indian Ocean, has described MCC as engaged in *translating* Christian service, a constant reinterpretation in new contexts of what "service in the name of Christ" looks like.[3] While Fountain's metaphor of translation has much to commend it, it also may unwittingly suggest that service in the name of Christ has a clear and stable meaning within Mennonite communities in the U.S. and Canada, with this fixed meaning then transposed into the varied contexts in which MCC operates.[4] The metaphor of construction more clearly captures that the meaning of Christian service (and of MCC's service in the name of Christ) is always fluid and is always being discerned, contested, and constructed anew, both in the U.S. and Canada and in diverse locations around the world. This ongoing process of constructing and contesting Christian service happens—or, better put, *takes place*— within specific landscapes, locations in a space-time matrix that people have invested with meanings, meanings that are historical and so always changing and shifting. People's locations have shaped how they have understood the call to "serve in the name of Christ," and service through MCC has in turn generated new terrains of spiritual kinship, new mappings of the church and of the identity of the neighbors and enemies whom Christians are called to serve.

A Personal Geography of MCC

As a way of making this theoretical argument more concrete, I share here some of my own personal MCC geography, charting the imagined landscapes constructed through my engagement with MCC from childhood until the present and examining how

---

[3] Philip Fountain, "Translating Christian Service: An Ethnography of the Mennonite Central Committee," Ph.D. diss., Australian National University, 2011.

[4] Fountain recognizes that translation is never a simple matter of transposing a fixed meaning from one language into a fixed meaning in another language, but rather represents a dynamic, fluid process of interpretation. My concern lies more with popular misunderstandings of the nature of translation.

these landscapes have shaped my understanding of Mennonites and Christian service. By referring to "imagined landscapes," I do not thereby suggest that the specific places through which my mental maps of MCC, Mennonites, and Christian service were formed were *imaginary*, as in non-existent. Rather, my invocation of imagined landscapes seeks to highlight two points: first, that encounters with places are historically mediated and ever-changing and thus are sites of potential contestation; and second, that it is through these historically constructed and negotiated encounters with places that individual and social identities are formed. Some markers, then, in my MCC landscape:

Fig. 7: Dianne Epp with students in Sundi-Lutete Secondary School, Congo, ca. 1967. (Photo used with permission from Dianne Epp)

My first remembered encounter with MCC was as a child in the basement of my family's home in Lincoln, Nebraska, in the 1970s, playing with the musical instruments my parents had brought back with them from a service term as newlyweds in the mid-1960s in what is now the Democratic Republic of the Congo. It was also in this basement that my parents occasionally set up the Kodak projector to present slide shows visualizing the two years they spent in the 1960s teaching Congolese high school students through MCC's Teachers Abroad Program (TAP) in a school founded by Swedish Protestant missionaries in the village of Sundi-Lutete (fig. 7).These slideshows simultaneously evoked in me a nostalgia for a past I did not personally experience and provoked a restless yearning to see a very different world beyond my white, middle-class Lincoln neighborhood, these projected images of Congolese people and landscapes nurturing a sense of service as adventure. Years later, I also wondered if these slideshows unwittingly fostered a racialized understanding of Christian service as something carried out by white Christians from the West to and for black and brown peoples around the globe.

A few years later in late grade school or early junior high, I stood in an exhibition hall at the county fairgrounds in Aurora, Nebraska, on the weekend of the Nebraska Mennonite Relief Sale, the proceeds from which went to support MCC's global efforts. I watched my uncle successfully bid on a commemorative MCC belt buckle. I ate my fill of the verenike

Fig. 8: Tri-County Relief Sale on Ralph Hertzler's farm outside Morgantown, Pennsylvania, ca. 1957-1959. (MCC photo/Burton Buller)

and farmer's sausage that were the culinary staples of my father's extended German-Russian family centered in Henderson, Nebraska. My father explained that the sale was operated not just by Mennonites from the General Conference Mennonite Church of my parents' families, but also by members of the Mennonite Brethren church in Henderson and the (Old) Mennonite church in Milford. This relief sale day reinforced my ethnic and religious identity; yet my time at the relief sale also broadened my map of the Mennonite landscape, introducing exotic new names and places for that map such as "Mennonite Brethren," "Old Mennonite," and "Milford." At this Nebraska MCC relief sale, service united people across divides of doctrine and practice, creating new maps of ecumenical cooperation (fig. 8).[5]

---

[5] Ervin Beck's study of the northern Indiana Michiana Mennonite Relief Sale in *MennoFolk: Mennonite and Amish Folk Traditions* (Scottdale, PA: Herald Press, 2004) discusses how MCC relief sales express, nurture, and reinforce ethnic

Around this time, I began weekly volunteering at Helping Hands Handicrafts, a new fair-trade venture in Lincoln that sold products from MCC's SELFHELP Crafts venture. SELFHELP Crafts had grown out of the initiative of Edna Ruth Byler in the 1950s to organize trunk shows in church basements of handicrafts from Puerto Rico and the West Bank (fig. 9). Helping Hands later became an MCC Ten Thousand Villages store.

Unpacking and selling soapstone dishes, jute basket hangers, and olive wood nativities connected me to artisans in Kenya, India, and the West Bank and to a vision of service as the promotion of global trade that pays producers a fair and living wage.[6]

A few years later, I sat in my family's living room, reading through a copy of the *Washington Office Memo*, published by MCC's office in Washington, D.C., search-

Fig. 9: Edna Ruth Byler with fair trade handicrafts in 1964. (MCC photo)

ing for material to use in high school debate and extemporaneous speech competitions. My mental map of MCC, Mennonites, and service expanded to include public policy advocacy in the halls of government power (fig. 10).[7]

identity. While valuable, Beck's study leaves insufficiently examined the extent to which relief sales also operate as sites of identity construction and contestation, with identities shifting over time.

[6] For assessments of SELFHELP Crafts and Ten Thousand Villages, see Jennifer Keahey, Mary Littrell, and Douglas Murray, "Business with a Mission: the Ongoing Role of Ten Thousand Villages within the Fair Trade Movement," in *A Table of Sharing: Mennonite Central Committee and the Expanding Networks of Mennonite Identity*, ed. Alain Epp Weaver (Telford, PA: Cascadia, 2010), 265-28; Laurel Zwissler, "Markets of the Heart: Weighing Economic and Ethical Values at Ten Thousand Villages," *Research in Economic Anthropology* 37 (2017): 115-135; and Keith R. Brown, "The Commodification of Altruism: Fair Trade and the Ethos of Ethical Consumption," Ph.D. diss., University of Pennsylvania, 2008.

[7] For accounts and evaluations of MCC's public policy advocacy work in

Fig. 10: MCC Washington Office director Delton Franz (right) with Senator Mark Hatfield at the twenty-fifth anniversary celebration of the MCC Washington office in 1993. (MCC photo/David Schrock-Shenk)

Several years later, my spouse and I began our lives as newlyweds in an apartment above a garage one block away from the Bethel campus in North Newton, Kansas. For suppers, we cooked through the pages of the *More-with-Less Cookbook*, compiled by MCC worker Doris Janzen Longacre and first published by MCC and Herald Press in 1976. These culinary explorations connected us to thousands of households across the U.S., Canada, and beyond that were also inspired by Janzen Longacre's vision of Christian service as bound up with domestic decisions, such as what and how to cook, a vision that linked Mennonite kitchens to global challenges of hunger, the just sharing of resources, and care for the environment (fig. 11).[8]

Ottawa and Washington, D.C., see William Janzen, *Advocating for Peace: Stories from the Ottawa Office of Mennonite Central Committee, 1975-2008* (Kitchener, ON: Pandora Press, 2020); Keith Graber Miller, *Wise as Serpents, Innocent as Doves: American Mennonites Engage Washington* (Knoxville, TN: University of Tennessee Press, 1996); and Rachelle Lyndaker Schlabach, "A Steady Witness for Peace: MCC in Washington, D.C.," *Intersections: MCC Theory and Practice Quarterly* 8, no. 3 (Summer 2020): 25-27.

[8] Janzen Longacre's *More-with-Less Cookbook* (Scottdale, PA: Herald Press, 1976) spawned an MCC/Herald Press series of World Community Cookbooks that included Joetta Handrich Schlabach, *Extending the Table* (Scottdale, PA: Herald Press, 1991) and Cathleen Hockman-Wert and Mary Beth Lind, *Simply in Season*

More-with-Less inspired later MCC publications that promoted simple living as a practical response to the iniquities of global capitalism and as a way of embodying faithful care for and harmony with the environment.[9] Since its publication more than forty years ago, the *More-with-Less* cookbook has sold over a million copies around the world, making it arguably the most effective outreach tool and most potent work of theology produced by twentieth-century Mennonites. A decade later, my spouse encountered a group of Israeli Jewish homeschooling mothers in Jerusalem who enthusiastically sang the praises of *More-with-Less*.

A year after college, my spouse and I moved to the small village of Zababdeh in the north of the occupied West Bank to teach English at a Catholic school. This initial three-year MCC assignment eventually expanded into a total of eleven years of work with Palestinians in the Occupied West Bank, Gaza Strip,

---

(Scottdale, PA: Herald Press, 2005). For analyses of the explicit and implicit theologies of this cookbook series, see Malinda Elizabeth Berry, "Extending the Theological Table: MCC's World Community Cookbooks as Organic Theology," in *A Table of Sharing: Mennonite Central Committee and the Expanding Networks of Mennonite Identity*, ed. Alain Epp Weaver (Telford, PA: Cascadia, 2010), 284-309; Matthew Bailey-Dick, "The Kitchenhood of All Believers: A Journey into the Discourse of Mennonite Cookbooks," *Mennonite Quarterly Review* 79, no. 2 (April 2005): 153–178; Cathleen Hockman-Wert, "Preaching the Good News with Our Mouths Full," *Vision: A Journal for Church and Theology* 9, no. 1 (Spring 2008): 69–75; and Kevin Stewart Rose, "'The World Food Crisis is Not a Fad': The *More-with-Less Cookbook* and Protestant Environmental Spirituality," *Religion and American Culture: A Journal of Interpretation* 29, no. 2 (July 2019): 216-254.

[9] Four years after the publication of *More-with-Less*, Janzen Longacre compiled a lifestyle guide to simple living as a companion to the *More-with-Less Cookbook*, appropriately entitled *Living More-with-Less* (Scottdale, PA: Herald Press, 1980). Over the ensuing three decades, MCC supported the creation of several additional publications that sought to foster simple Christian living and care for the environment, including Art and Jocele Meyer, *Earthkeepers: Environmental Perspectives on Hunger, Poverty, and Injustice* (Scottdale: PA: Herald Press, 1991); David Schrock-Shenk, ed, *Basic Trek: Venture into a World of Enough* (Scottdale, PA: Herald Press, 2002); Jeanne Jantzi, *Parent Trek: Nurturing Creativity and Care in Our Children* (Scottdale, PA: Herald Press, 2001); and Joanne Moyer, *Earth Trek: Celebrating and Sustaining God's Creation* (Scottdale, PA: Herald Press, 2004). For an overview of these publications and MCC sustainability initiatives during the past half century, see Meara Kwee, "MCC Creation Care and Sustainability Initiatives over the Decades," *Intersections: MCC Theory and Practice Quarterly* 8, no. 2 (Spring 2020): 19-21.

Fig. 11: MCC staff member Doris Janzen Longacre and her daughter Cara Sue Longacre demonstrate preparing a garden vegetable and ground beef dish by the Chinese stir-fry method at a seminar in 1976. Janzen Longacre's More-with-Less Cookbook was first published in 1976. (MCC photo/Ernie Klassen)

and East Jerusalem. Sent by MCC to the olive tree-covered hills of the northern West Bank and the cramped cinder block homes of Gaza's refugee camps, our MCC administrators instructed us that Christian service was less about classes to teach or reports to write and more about *presence*, about sitting under our landlord's fig tree to drink cup after cup of sage-flavored tea and slowly learning to communicate in Arabic (fig. 12). Over the course of a decade drinking countless cups of tea and coffee with neighbors, co-workers, and friends in a context of military occupation, our imagined landscape of Christian service expanded and became more complex, as we learned that Christian service as peacebuilding demanded ecumenical and interfaith collaboration as well as advocacy for unpopular causes.[10]

Fig. 12: Sonia Weaver and Alain Epp Weaver enjoying supper with friends in the Deir el-Balah refugee camp in the Gaza Strip in the fall of 1999. (Photo courtesy of Alain Epp Weaver)

---

[10] From speaking in churches with slide shows and later powerpoints to writing articles and books for the church press and academic audiences, MCC staff have sought over the decades to advocate for a just future for all in Palestine-Israel, advocacy rooted in over 70 years of accompaniment of Palestinian refugees, the Palestinian churches, and Palestinians and Israeli Jews struggling nonviolently for a just peace in the land. Select publications written by MCC staff or supported by MCC about Palestine-Israel over the decades include: Frank H. Epp, *Whose Land is Palestine? The Middle East in Historical Perspective* (Grand Rapids, MI: Wm. B. Eerdmans, 1974); John A. Lapp, *The View from East Jerusalem* (Scottdale, PA: Herald Press, 1980); Sonia K. Weaver, *What is Palestine-Israel? Answers to Common Questions* (Scottdale, PA: Herald Press, 2007); and Alain Epp Weaver, ed., *Under Vine and Fig Tree: Biblical Theologies of Land and the Palestinian-Israeli Conflict* (Telford, PA: Cascadia, 2007).

Finally, a little over a decade ago, we moved to Lancaster County in southeastern Pennsylvania, where I began an administrative job with MCC at its U.S. headquarters in the quiet township of Akron. The same small village where MCC leader Orie Miller operated a shoe factory, Akron occupies a place on the Mennonite world map much larger than its actual size.[11] Over the past decade, I have welcomed long-time MCC workers and partner representatives from countries like Nigeria, Zambia, India, and Indonesia who express surprise upon their arrival in Pennsylvania that Akron, which in some Mennonite mental landscapes functions as the Vatican of the global Mennonite world, is simply a sleepy, quiet township of a few thousand people, not a bustling urban center like Jos, Nigeria, or Lusaka, Zambia, but a hamlet where one awakens to the clip-clop of horses on the street pulling Amish buggies. From the vantage point of an administrator in Akron, my mapping of the MCC world yields less the command-and-control organizational chart of a modern corporation, with Akron in the center or at the top, but more a rhizome-like network in which MCC keeps expanding outward in increasingly complex ways from multiple nodes.

MCC's Complex Landscapes of Service

I did not map my personal geography of MCC because it is broadly representative or comprehensively descriptive. Quite the opposite: I detailed my personal MCC landscape precisely because of its fragmentary, individual character, to highlight that there is not simply one MCC story of service in the name of Christ, but many. Readers of this book represent diverse geographies of MCC service and this diversity comprises but a small part of MCC's global landscapes. Even as MCC has operated to create new types of Anabaptist-Mennonite identity and shared understandings of Christian service, one's encounter with MCC and one's understanding of service in the name of Christ are nevertheless powerfully shaped by the formative

---

[11] For an account of Miller's work with MCC over half a century, see chapters 4 through 9 of John Sharp, *My Calling to Fulfill: The Orie O. Miller Story* (Harrisonburg, VA: Herald Press, 2015).

Fig. 13: Linie Friesen (front) and Sara Stoesz (back), who along with Selma Loewen and Susan Giesbrecht founded the first thrift MCC shop in Altona, Manitoba, in 1972, are pictured in 2012 in the Altona MCC Gift and Thrift Shop during a fortieth anniversary celebration of the store's opening. (MCC photo/Anthony J. Siemens)

landscapes one inhabits, including landscapes of national, religious, racial, and gendered identity.

MCC landscapes of service can vary significantly just within the relatively limited geography of southeastern Pennsylvania where I live and work: from meat canning events organized on farms by Old Order Amish and Mennonite districts, to youth groups from Hmong and Nepali Mennonite churches volunteering at MCC's material resources center in Ephrata, to the placements of young adults from Africa, Asia, and Latin America in one-year service assignments at Mennonite schools in Lancaster County, to recent graduates of the Brethren in Christ college, Messiah, leaving the United States for a year of service in countries like Honduras, Lebanon, and Mozambique.

This diversity of MCC geographies of service expands and becomes more complex as one zooms out from southeastern Pennsylvania to take a global view. An unrepresentative sampling of the global landscapes of MCC service could include: a Church of God in Christ, Mennonite, woman in central Kansas who pieces and knots comforters that will be shipped globally for distribution to displaced families; a retired Mennonite Brethren man in Abbotsford, British Columbia, who volunteers at an MCC thrift store; a Muslim woman in Kolkata, India, who for decades has coordinated MCC's educational partnerships; a young man from a Low German Mennonite colony in Paraguay's Chaco region spending two years traveling across the United States and Canada while working on MCC's mobile meat canner; a Protestant Nigerian man who has led interfaith peacebuilding efforts in several African countries and who now leads MCC's program in Zimbabwe; and a Cambodian Mennonite woman working for a year on forestation and food security projects in Haiti's Artibonite Valley. One could easily come up with hundreds, even thousands, more snapshots of global MCC landscapes, each opening a vista onto what service in the name of Christ looks like, each distinct while also bearing some similarities to one another. Taking a global view reveals MCC as a complex, shifting field of interconnecting, sometimes overlapping landscapes of service, with MCC service creating new, imagined landscapes of identity and connection. MCC's complex network of rhizome-like connections is shaped and changed in turn by new challenges to and discoveries about Christian service within different geographies.

Fig. 14: A group of meat canning volunteers from Hutchinson, Kansas, in 2018 label cans of chicken after the cans have been sealed and wiped down. (MCC photo/Josh Voth)

Recounting MCC's complex, hundred-year history, as I seek to do in this book, could proceed by focusing on a wide variety of MCC landscapes, examining the questions those landscapes have raised for MCC about the nature of Christian service. One could, for example, map the terrain of practical inter-Mennonite ecumenism created through MCC. MCC relief sales, thrift shops (fig. 13), mobile meat canning events (fig. 14), and material resources centers: at these places, inter-Mennonite connections and expanded understandings of Anabaptist-Mennonite identity through collaboration in service have been forged. During World War II, MCC-administered Civilian Public Service camps not only brought Mennonite young men and women with diverse theological commitments together to carry out alternative service to war, they also operated as educational venues in which MCC sought to strengthen the religious identity of Mennonite young adults through the distribution of specially commissioned pamphlets on Mennonite history and theology and through the organization of educational events. Following World War II, as MCC Pax men carried out alternative service obligations through relief and reconstruction efforts in post-war Europe, MCC sought to nurture and reinforce an inter-Mennonite commitment to nonresistance, organizing regular conferences about the meaning of Christian peace witness. Meanwhile, MCC's oldest partner globally is Mennonite World Conference, a worldwide fellowship of Anabaptist churches founded only five years after MCC in 1925.[12] To be sure, inter-Mennonite cooperation through MCC has often proven fragile, with some churches wary, even at MCC's beginnings, of too close collaboration with one another and with conflicts over doctrine, ethics, and visions of Christian service testing commitment to inter-Mennonite partnership.[13] Yet, even amidst such conflict, MCC has worked to nurture readiness among Mennonite churches with markedly different theological and ethical visions to set aside those differences to cooperate on concrete tasks. Over the decades, MCC administrators and board members have found that this commitment to inter-Mennonite collaboration is

---

[12] For an historical overview and analysis of the interrelationship between MCC and Mennonite World Conference, see Ronald J.R. Mathies, "Synergies in Mission: MCC and Mennonite World Conference," in *A Table of Sharing: Mennonite Central Committee and the Expanding Networks of Mennonite Identity*, ed. Alain Epp Weaver (Telford, PA: Cascadia, 2010), 84-103.

[13] For an account of the inter-Mennonite tensions negotiated at MCC's founding, see James C. Juhnke, "Turning Points, Broken Ice, and *Glaubensgenossen*: What Happened at Prairie Street on July 27-28, 1920?" in *A Table of Sharing: Mennonite Central Committee and the Expanding Networks of Mennonite Identity*, ed. Alain Epp Weaver (Telford, PA: Cascadia, 2010), 66-83.

never fully solidified, but must always be tended, reinforced, and won anew.[14]

Another way to map MCC's story would to be explore how MCC has operated within and been shaped by landscapes of war and revolution, from distribution of emergency relief supplies to displaced peoples in post-World War II Europe, to service programs carried out in Vietnam in the midst of the U.S.-led war in the country, to community development workers placed in rural communities in El Salvador and Nicaragua during times of revolutionary unrest and U.S.-backed military repression, to partnerships for relief today with Syrian churches seeking to show Christ's love in practical ways to the millions of Syrians uprooted by the ongoing civil war. Within such landscapes, MCC has encountered questions such as: How does Christian service look like and differ from military service? What types of cooperation and coordination with governments and militaries are justifiable for a Christian organization committed to nonviolence as it carries out relief and development programs? What does Christian peace witness look like "behind enemy lines"?[15] Are Mennonites called to advocate to the governments of the United States and Canada not only for conscientious objection status, but also against the globalized militarism of these states? What does Christ-like presence among and solidarity with oppressed and marginalized peoples look like within revolutionary contexts, in which one's neighbors, including one's Christian neighbors, are sympathetic to

---

[14] Sociologist Donald Kraybill analyzes the surprising resilience of broad-based support for MCC across the Anabaptist continuum in the United States in "The Mystery of Broad-Based Commitment: MCC in the Eyes of Mennonites and Brethren in Christ in the United States," in *A Table of Sharing: Mennonite Central Committee and the Expanding Networks of Mennonite Identity*, ed. Alain Epp Weaver (Telford, PA: Cascadia, 2010), 105-134. Steve Nolt, meanwhile, examines MCC connections with plain Anabaptist groups in "MCC's Relationship with 'Plain' Anabaptists in Historical Perspective," in *A Table of Sharing: Mennonite Central Committee and the Expanding Networks of Mennonite Identity*, ed. Alain Epp Weaver (Telford, PA: Cascadia, 2010), 135-166.

[15] See reflections from MCC workers placed over the decades in "enemy" contexts such as Eastern Europe during the Cold War, Iran, Afghanistan, North Korea, and Iraq in "Peacebuilding as Presence: MCC Assignments in 'Enemy' Contexts," *Intersections: MCC Theory and Practice Quarterly* 8, no. 3 (Summer 2020): 54-63.

revolution (fig. 15)? How can Christians work constructively at conflict transformation and restorative justice not only globally but in the United States and Canada as well?[16]

Or one could tell MCC's story of service in the name of Christ by mapping landscapes of forced displacement and migration and MCC's operations within such landscapes, from MCC's decision in 1949 to establish a relief and rehabilitation unit amidst the Palestinian refugee camps around Jericho in the Jordanian-controlled West Bank following the Arab-Israeli war that displaced two-thirds of the Palestinian population, to MCC Canada responding to the so-called Vietnamese "boat people" crisis by negotiating with the Canadian government in the late 1970s to allow Mennonite congregations to sponsor Vietnamese refugees for resettlement as newcomers to Canada, to MCC accompanying a community like Mampuján in Colombia as it sought justice and compensation after a massacre in the village in 2002 led to the village's abandonment (fig. 16), to MCC today working with churches and community-based groups along the Mexico-U.S. borderlands to support asylum seekers and other new migrants from Central America.[17] Mennonites of European background have often narrated their histories as ones of displacement and migration in the search for religious freedom and liberty. Through MCC, Mennonites in Canada and the U.S. have been confronted with the role of nation-states such as their own in directly and indirectly creating mass displacement and

---

[16] Michelle Armster offers an overview of how MCC's Conciliation Service and its successors in the United States sought to address these questions in "Mennonite Conciliation Service: Challenges, Successes, and Learnings," *Intersections: MCC Theory and Practice Quarterly* 8, no. 3 (Summer 2020): 32-35. Mennonite Conciliation Service (MCS) captured and promoted learnings from its efforts in its widely-used training manuals. See Carolyn Schrock-Shenk, ed., *Mediation and Facilitation Training Manual: Foundations and Skills for Constructive Conflict Transformation*, fourth edition (Akron, PA: Mennonite Conciliation Service, 2000) and Lorraine Stutzman Amstutz and Michelle Armster, eds., *Conflict Transformation and Restorative Justice Manual: Foundations and Skills for Mediation and Facilitation*, fifth edition (Akron, PA: MCC Office on Justice and Peacebuilding, 2008).

[17] For an analysis of the origins of MCC Canada's refugee resettlement program, see William Janzen, "The MCC Canada 1979 Master Agreement for the Sponsorship of Refugees in Historical Perspective," *Journal of Mennonite Studies* 24 (2006): 211-222.

Fig. 15: This 1975 photo shows Max Ediger, James Klassen, Earl Martin, and Yoshihiro Ichikawa, MCC workers who remained in Saigon following the withdrawal of U.S. troops from Vietnam. (Photo courtesy of Earl Martin)

with how Jesus' command to visit prisoners, feed the hungry, and give water to the thirsty calls them to place welcoming refugees, asylum seekers, and migrants above nationalist politics of exclusion and militarized borders.

The landscapes that have shaped the MCC story are numerous and diverse: multiple books could be written simply seeking to enumerate and describe all the landscapes in which the story of MCC service in the name of Christ has taken shape over a century. For the rest of this chapter, I look more closely at one specific way to map the MCC story, namely, through an analysis of the colonial, racialized, and decolonizing landscapes that have shaped and continue to shape MCC's service in the name of Christ.

Colonial, Racialized, and Decolonial Landscapes of Service

Most of the contexts in which MCC has operated have been shaped by ongoing legacies of colonialism, be it how transatlantic trafficking in enslaved humans from Africa helped to form the United States since well before its independence, or through the settler colonialism practiced in the United States, Canada, South Africa, or Israel-Palestine, or through the extractive colonialism undertaken by the United Kingdom in countries like India, Kenya, and Rhodesia (now Zimbabwe),

Fig. 16: In this 2010 photo, Viviana Meza Guerra (right) and Yaqueline Morelno Morales hang a vibrantly colored quilt that documents the violence and displacement their Colombian community of Mampuján has experienced. MCC accompanied the community as they pressed for justice. (MCC photo/Silas Crews)

Belgium in what is now the Democratic Republic of the Congo, the French in places like Chad and Burkina Faso, the Portuguese in Mozambique and Brazil, and the Spanish across Latin America. How have these legacies of colonialism shaped MCC's understanding and practice of Christian service? To what extent have MCC understandings and practice of Christian service embodied colonialism's racialized value hierarchies, with a white, resource-rich, and advanced Christian West going out to serve among Indigenous, black, and brown peoples in the global South marked by need and portrayed as less advanced at best and as primitive or savage at worst? How can an organization like MCC work deliberately to decolonize its practice of Christian service, to free itself of captivity to colonial understandings of service marked by a condescending, unilateral, and often racialized movement of service *from* the global North *to* the global South and, in that process, discover different models of service?

These questions are not new within MCC—I circle back to these types of questions throughout the ensuing chapters. In chapter 3, I trace debates within MCC from the early 1970s into the 1980s that led to a redefinition of service as presence, listening, and mutual sharing, while in chapter 5, I examine

MCC critiques in the 1970s and 1980s of modernization's development discourses that replicated colonial value hierarchies and MCC's attempts to identify alternative models of development. In the remainder of this chapter, I consider some of the colonial and racialized landscapes of service in MCC's history as well as some of the ways MCC has sought to participate in the decolonization of those landscapes.[18]

The vocabulary of colonies and colonization can be traced to MCC's early history. Alongside MCC's first relief response in the 1920s among starving Mennonites and their neighbors in the parts of Russia once home to the Mennonite colonies of Khortitza and Molotschna, Mennonites in the U.S. and Canada organized what they termed boards of colonization to prepare for the potential settlement of Mennonite immigrants from Russia in the plains states and provinces. With immigration barred to the U.S., only the Canadian Mennonite Board of Colonization, in collaboration with the Canadian Pacific Railway, ended up settling Mennonite immigrants in the early 1920s, settling them on land the Canadian government had cleared by extinguishing Indigenous land claims through treaties. As Esther Epp-Tiessen explains, the Canadian Mennonite Board of Colonization, one of the precursor agencies to what became MCC Canada, often portrayed the land on which these new Mennonite immigrants from the Soviet Union settled as an empty promised land of opportunities, the Indigenous history of the land erased from view.[19]

MCC's second major initiative involved assistance to Mennonite refugees fleeing the Soviet Union in colonizing the Paraguayan Chaco between 1930 and 1932, after the Paraguayan government had made land in the Chaco available for settlement, the traditional lands on which the nomadic,

---

[18] For analyses of historical and contemporary intersections of Anabaptism and colonialism, see the articles in the "Anabaptism and Colonialism" issue of MCC's *Peace Office Newsletter* 41, no. 3 (Summer 2011) and the "Legacies of Colonialism" issue of *Intersections: MCC Theory and Practice Quarterly* 2, no. 1 (Winter 2014).

[19] Esther Epp-Tiessen, "Mennonites Colonizing Canada and the United States," *Intersections: MCC Theory and Practice Quarterly* 2, no. 1 (Winter 2014): 13-14.

Indigenous Enxet and Nivaclé people hunted and gathered.[20] A twenty-fifth anniversary history about and by MCC in 1945 presented this colonization enterprise as an "epic" story, a story recounted by the author in racialized terms that praised Mennonites for proving that "white men" could settle in the Chaco and that paired "wild animals" and "unfriendly Indians" as examples of the threats Mennonite settlers faced. The dramatic prose in this silver anniversary booklet likened the "ten-thousand-mile pilgrimage by two thousand penniless refugees" to the journey of the Israelites to the Promised Land as well as to the conquest of the plains by "the American frontiersmen who crossed the Alleghenies after the Revolution." The booklet's author described these Mennonite immigrants to the Chaco as facing a "primitive and unsettled" "wilderness": by "unsettled," one must hasten to add, the author meant settled by Europeans, for the author soon refers to the presence of "aboriginal Indians." Observing that "skeptics had claimed" that the Chaco "was impossible to settle," the author recounted with pride and admiration that "in less than twenty-five years' time they [Mennonites] have demonstrated beyond doubt what Paraguay failed to accomplish in over four hundred years of control—that white men can live and make a living in the interior of the Chaco. They survived plague and pests, wild animals and unfriendly Indians, the rigours of a strange, semi-tropical climate and the trials of adjustment to a totally different type of agriculture, the perils of internal dissension and the problems of inaccessible markets. Like Caesar," the author concluded, "[the Mennonite settlers] came, they saw, and they conquered—but peacefully."[21]

---

[20] Historical accounts of Mennonite colonization in Paraguay include: J. Winfield Fretz, *Pilgrims in Paraguay: The Story of Mennonite Colonization in South America* (Scottdale, PA: Herald Press, 1953); Edgar Stoesz and Muriel T. Stackley, *Garden in the Wilderness: Mennonite Communities in the Paraguayan Chaco* (Winnipeg: CMBC, 1999); and various writings by Peter P. Klassen, such as *Die Mennoniten in Paraguay: Reich Gottes und Reich dieser Welt*, vol. 1, second edition (Bolanden-Weierhof, Germany: Mennonitischer Geschichtsverein e.V. 2001) and *Die Mennoniten in Paraguay: Begegnung mit Indianern und Paraguayern*, vol. 2 (Bolanden-Weierhof: Mennonitischer Geschichtsverein e.V. 1991).

[21] *Twenty-Five Years: 1920-1945* (Akron, PA: Mennonite Central Committee, 1945), 10.

Frontier colonial projects have used the construction of transportation systems such as railroads and roads to expand the reach of state control. In the late 1950s, more than 50 MCC Pax men worked and lived alongside Paraguayan Mennonites and Paraguayan soldiers as they constructed the Trans-Chaco highway that connected the Chaco with the Paraguayan capital of Asunción (fig. 17). For Paraguayan Mennonites, the 250-mile highway, completed in 1961, represented an economic lifeline to Paraguay's economic heart, while for the Paraguayan state the highway furthered its project of internal colonial expansion and control.

As Paraguayan Mennonites solidified their presence in the Chaco, with close accompaniment from MCC, they developed a vision of a civilizing mission that would reach out to the Chaco's Indigenous peoples. Hans Epp, a Paraguayan Mennonite from the Fernheim colony and long-time medical missionary among the Indigenous peoples of the Chaco, shared with the MCC board in 1973 that Paraguayan Mennonites took their encounter with the Lengua (Enxet) tribe "as being by divine providence." Epp sought to distance Mennonites from responsibility for the precarious plight of the Indigenous people of the Chaco, stressing that "The Mennonites did not come to the Chaco because of the Indians. They had legally purchased the land and their biggest desire was to live free, peaceful and according to the dictates of their conscience. They were looking for a new home." However, Epp continued, upon meeting the Lengua and seeing "many of their struggles and their problems," Paraguayan Mennonites organized a multifaceted mission of evangelization, the promotion of modern farming techniques, and education and health initiatives, a mission they named *Licht den Indianern* or "Light to the Indians."[22]

---

[22] Hans E. Epp, "Indians in the Paraguayan Chaco: A Challenge," MCC Annual Meeting, January 19-20, 1973, 94, in the folder Docuware/Binational (BN) Minutes & Meeting Packets 1920 to 2012, Mennonite Central Committee Executive Committee Meeting Minutes, #361, January 19-20, 1973, Exhibit 8, 92-96, MCC U.S. archives, Akron, Pennsylvania.

In contrast, other MCC discourse around colonization erased Indigenous presence from view. In 1945, in the context of discussions about developing more formalized and institutionalized Mennonite mutual aid mechanisms, including for young men completing alternative service commitments during World War II through the MCC-administered Civilian

Fig. 17: MCC Pax worker John J. Kauffman, from Iowa City, Iowa, adjusts the clutch while the Paraguayan grease crew works on the Caterpillar D7 bulldozer along the Trans-Chaco highway on November 12, 1960. (MCC photo)

Public Service (CPS) program, MCC commissioned J. Winfield Fretz, then a professor of sociology at Bethel College, to write a booklet about Mennonite colonization efforts.[23] Fretz sought in that study to identify factors that strengthened or weakened community cohesion as Mennonites migrated from place to place, with the purpose of making recommendations for resettling CPS workers following their service. Fretz left the role of the state in settler-colonial projects practically unaddressed. Strikingly absent from Fretz's discussion of Mennonite colonization in the plains of the United States and Canada in the 1870s was any acknowledgment of the Indigenous people who had previously lived on the land or of the role of state power in

---

[23] J. Winfield Fretz, *Mennonite Colonization: Lessons from the Past for the Future* (Akron, PA: Mennonite Central Committee, 1944). See also Fretz, *Mennonite Colonization in Mexico* (Akron, PA: Mennonite Central Committee, 1945).

clearing Indigenous people from the land as a prelude to opening it up for colonization by white settlers of European descent. Fretz would have been aware of the prior Indigenous histories of places such Goessel (Kansas), Henderson (Nebraska), Freeman (South Dakota), or Steinbach (Manitoba), making the absence of reference to Indigenous peoples in his booklet about Mennonite colonization stand out all the more.

Colonial legacies have also shaped MCC service programs. The potentially colonial character of Christian service was not foreign to the young adults from the U.S. and Canada sent by MCC through its Teachers Abroad Program (TAP) in the sixties and early seventies to help staff government and Protestant mission schools in newly independent African countries, countries which sought to chart new paths of independence from former colonial powers while also turning to the educational systems inherited by the colonial powers as vital tools for freedom and development. MCC placed TAP teachers in countries such as Nigeria, Congo, Kenya, and Malawi that had recently emerged from direct colonial control. Some of these MCC workers struggled with what these colonial legacies meant for Christian service. Ken Lohrentz, a TAP worker in Tanzania in the early 1960s, observed that new TAP teachers should expect to "come in contact with some expatriates whose attitudes about Africans, and the corresponding thoughts they express, follow the channels of colonial attitudes rather closely," warning these new MCC workers that without deliberate, conscious effort, they would find themselves adopting a colonial mindset as well.[24]

Fig. 18: Anthony Epp, participant in MCC's Teachers Abroad Program (TAP), with a student at Sundi-Lutete Secondary School in Congo. 1967. (Photo courtesy of Anthony Epp)

---

[24] Ken Lohrentz, "Attitudes of the TAP Teacher," February 1965. IX-12-04, box

However, disentangling themselves from the colonial legacies of the countries in which they served proved challenging for TAP teachers, especially when these MCC workers lived and worked within colonial structures. In an April 1966 report about his TAP assignment at a Swedish Protest mission school in Sundi-Lutete north of Matadi in Congo, Anthony Epp wrote of the awkwardness of living in "'the white camp,' as the students so aptly call our segregated part of the mission post," observing that "it is really difficult to enjoy the comforts of a nice house when one knows that one has such comforts because one has a white skin and when one learns that money which had been set aside to improve student quarters has been poured into the construction of one's own comfortable house. Several times recently we have encountered the astounding philosophy that it is only natural to look after housing needs of white teachers before those of the Congolese who are already used to living in poor conditions. It is on hearing such attitudes from 'missionaries' that one begins to understand why missionaries are not always loved."[25] A month later, Epp shared that he and his spouse had made conscious efforts to invite students and Congolese teachers over to eat in their part of the mission post and had in turn been invited by Congolese to eat with them (fig. 18). Epp reported that "time and again, the remark comes back" that "we were so happy to have you eat with us, for we are accustomed to having the Europeans bring their own food and go off to eat separately. One really gets the impression," Epp continued, "that in being made Christians these people have, in a sense, been somewhat dehumanized. Perhaps we will be able to make a contribution in this area, at least we are trying to do so."[26]

#9, folder #17, folder title "Teachers Abroad Program 1965-1966," MCC U.S. archives, Akron, Pennsylvania.

[25] Anthony and Dianne Epp, "Progress Report—March 1966," April 2, 1966, 1, IX-06-03, box #198, folder #116/138, folder title "MCC Correspondence 1966-Teachers Abroad Program Activity Reports," MCC U.S. archives, Akron, Pennsylvania.

[26] Anthony R. Epp progress report "MCC Report—April 1966," May 5, 1966, 1, IX-06-03, Box #198, Folder #116/138, folder title "MCC Correspondence 1966-Teachers Abroad Program Activity Reports," MCC U.S. archives, Akron, Pennsylvania.

Over the ensuing decade, MCC would increasingly seek to place MCC workers in assignments outside of mission compound walls and with a stress on sharing daily life with the everyday people whom one had come to serve—eating and drinking tea with them, celebrating and mourning with them, and becoming conversant in local languages rather than colonial languages. As will be discussed further in the next chapter, unidirectional models of service gave way within MCC to understandings of service as mutual sharing and as multi-directional. This shift in how service was understood went hand-in-hand with two other developments that began to emerge from the 1980s onwards. First, MCC began to reflect more explicitly on the essential role of in-country nationals in carrying out its relief, development, and peacebuilding service and to grapple with what truly equitable intercultural service teams might look like.[27] Second, with the rise of civil society institutions across countries in the global South, MCC's primary mode of operation shifted from direct implementation to partnership with churches and other local organizations, partnerships that MCC hoped would be marked by what it called "mutual transformation." I return in chapter 5 to a closer examination of the rhetoric of mutual transformation.

Meanwhile, workers in MCC Voluntary Service units in Canada and the United States came face-to-face with the colonial and racialized characters of their own countries. In the United States, workers in MCC Voluntary Service units in places such as Gulfport, Mississippi (founded in 1946 alongside a Civilian Public Service camp), and Atlanta, Georgia (led during part of

---

[27] MCC workers from within the global contexts in which MCC operates have played essential roles within and provided much-needed linguistic, cultural, and contextual knowledge and operational continuity for MCC programs, yet popular and academic accounts of MCC have given inadequate attention to how these staff have shaped MCC's work and witness. This book is no exception, drawing primarily on the reports, working papers, and other writings of MCC staff from the global North. Another MCC history waits to be written that would narrate MCC's history from the perspective of these MCC workers. For reflections from some of the in-country nationals who have provided decades-long leadership for MCC's global programs, see "Assessing the Evolution of MCC's Development Work: Reflections from MCC Staff," *Intersections: MCC Theory and Practice Quarterly* 8, no. 2 (Spring 2020): 12-19.

the 1960s by civil rights leaders Vincent and Rosemarie Harding), were confronted by the stark racial discrimination of the Jim Crow South (fig. 19).[28] MCC workers placed among First Nations communities in Canada came face-to-face with Canada's colonial history, including its dispossession of Indigenous peoples, slowly learning the hard yet ultimately hopeful reality that reconciliation between Indigenous and settler Canadians requires truth-telling and justice (fig. 20).[29]

Over time, MCC also began to reckon with the fact that the colonial legacies of dispossession and racism in the United States and Canada were not simply external to MCC and to Mennonite communities in the two countries. MCC U.S.'s Damascus Road anti-racism program, founded in the 1990s, took the lead in highlighting that the white supremacist project that had shaped the United States from its origins had also shaped Mennonite churches and communities and MCC itself.[30] Such anti-racist

---

[28] For an examination of the Hardings' time with Mennonites, including with MCC, see Tobin Miller Shearer, "Moving beyond Charisma in Civil Rights Scholarship: Vincent Harding's Sojourn with the Mennonites, 1958-1966," *Mennonite Quarterly Review* 82, no. 2 (April 2008): 213-248.

[29] See Neil Funk Unrau, "Exploring the Gap between Mennonite and Indigenous Neighbours: Snapshots from the Story of Native Concerns, Mennonite Central Committee Canada," *Conrad Grebel Review* 29, no. 1 (2011): 52-57, for an historical examination of MCC Canada's Native Concerns (later Indigenous Neighbours) program. See also Anna Vogt, "MCC Advocacy for Indigenous Rights in Canada: Reflections from History and the Present," *Intersections: MCC Theory and Practice Quarterly* 8, no. 3 (Summer 2020): 28-31.

[30] In addition to operating the Damascus Road program, MCC U.S. anti-racism staff also published extensively, including Tobin Miller Shearer, *Enter the River: Healing Steps from White Privilege toward Racial Reconciliation* (Scottdale, PA: Herald Press, 1994) and Iris de León-Hartshorn, Tobin Miller Shearer, and Regina Shands Stoltzfus, *Set Free: A Journey toward Solidarity against Racism* (Scottdale, PA: Herald Press, 2001). For historical analysis of the Damascus Road program, see Iris de León-Hartshorn, "The Hard Work of Anti-Racism: The Good, the Bad, and the Ugly," *Intersections: MCC Theory and Practice Quarterly* 8, no. 3 (Summer 2020): 35-37; Tobin Miller Shearer, "Whitening Conflicts: White Racial Identity Formation within Mennonite Central Committee, 1960-1986," in *A Table of Sharing: Mennonite Central Committee and the Expanding Networks of Mennonite Identity*, ed. Alain Epp Weaver (Telford, PA: Cascadia, 2010), 215-238; and Tobin Miller Shearer, "White Mennonite Peacemakers: Oxymorons, Grace, and Nearly Thirty Years of Talking about Whiteness," *Conrad Grebel Review* 35, no. 3 (Fall 2017): 259-266.

Fig. 19: In this September 1963 photo, David Augsburger interviews Dr. Vincent Harding (left) on the Mennonite Hour. Together with his wife Rosemarie, Harding led the Atlanta (Georgia) Mennonite Service Unit in the early 1960s. (MCC photo)

analysis has underscored that disentangling MCC service from colonial mindsets and patterns is not a simple one-time decision, but instead an ongoing process of commitment and discernment.

In 2016, Eileen Klassen Hamm reflected on a long process undertaken by MCC Saskatchewan related to legacies of colonialism in Canada. In 1897, the Canadian government unilaterally took over land allotted by treaty to the Young Chippewayan Band to use for European settlement. This land includes a hill sacred to the Young Chippewayan, which they call Opwashemoe Chakatinaw. German-speaking Mennonites and Lutherans from what is now Ukraine then settled on this land, farmed, raised families, and passed down title deeds issued by the Canadian government within their families. Members of the Young Chippewayan Band, meanwhile, have passed on stories and traditions associated with Opwashemoe Chakatinaw from generation to generation, along with a claim of a violated treaty. For more than two decades, MCC has accompanied members of these Mennonite, Lutheran, and Young Chippewayan First Nation communities in discussing what justice and reconciliation might look like on the land they all love and call home. These conversations, Klassen Hamm

Fig. 20: Photographed in 2011, Elizabeth (Tshaukuish) Penashue, an Innu elder from Sheshatshiu, north of Happy Valley Goose Bay, Newfoundland, leads an annual canoe trip, supported by MCC, to increase awareness of the importance of protecting land and water from pollution and to pass on knowledge of Innu culture, traditional survival skills, and Innu foodways. (MCC photo/Nina Linton)

observes, have not been simple. They have required time, patience, commitment, and, for the Mennonite and Lutheran settlers, the humility to listen and sit with ambiguity. "We as settlers need to return again and again to humble learning," Klassen Hamm emphasizes. "We continue to want to control and manage the process. We still think we know what is best."[31]

Klassen Hamm's admonition for a return again and again to humble learning is good counsel for MCC as it embarks on a second century of service in the name of Christ. A centennial, to be sure, represents a time for celebration and thanksgiving to God. Yet Christian service through relief, development, and peacebuilding efforts is, like all human affairs, complicated, at times messy and ambiguous, and sometimes deeply flawed and

---

[31] Eileen Klassen Hamm, "Overcoming the Doctrine of Discovery at Opwashemoe Chakatinaw/Stoney Knoll," *Intersections: MCC Theory and Practice Quarterly* 6, no. 1 (Winter 2018), 8. MCC Saskatchewan supported production of the 2016 film about the Indigenous-settler encounter at Opwashemoe Chakatinaw, *Reserve 107: Reconciliation on the Prairies*, produced by Rebel Sky Media, available at https://www.reserve107thefilm.com/. See also Alain Epp Weaver, "Planting Trees in Exile," in *Yours, Mine, Ours: Unravelling the Doctrine of Discovery*, ed. Steven Heinrichs and Cheryl Woelk (Winnipeg: CommonWord, 2016), 108-110.

marked by failure. The optimism animating much humanitarian action can sometimes result in humanitarianism becoming a form of uncritical triumphalism. That impulse can certainly be found in MCC's hundred-year history. Yet MCC has also undertaken a patient, non-triumphalist form of Christian service, a form of Christian service that relinquishes the need for unilateral control, a form of Christian service that instead patiently sits with churches and local organizations to discern how best to work together at the tasks of relief, development, and peacebuilding, a form of Christian service that does not map a terrain to be controlled, but rather enters a landscape of mutual hospitality and sharing.

Chapter 3: Listening and Waiting: Shifting Understandings of Service in MCC

What is service? What constitutes Christian service? What does it mean to serve the church and the world? The concept of service has stood at the heart of MCC's self-identity for decades, with the motto "service in the name of Christ" core to its identity. Yet, at the same time, service has had multiple meanings over MCC's nearly century-long history. Or, perhaps better put, the nature of service has been an ongoing point of contestation within MCC. In this chapter, I trace shifting meanings of service across MCC's history, examining how MCC workers have critiqued and reimagined service. This chapter also asks who we imagine when we think of people engaged in Christian service. Do we imagine MCC workers as white citizens of the United States or Canada, the descendants of German-speaking Mennonites from Europe, such as myself and many others whom I quote in this book? How constrained and limited are our visions of Christian service? Such questions will weave in and out of this and following chapters as I reflect on MCC's century of service in the name of Christ.

Service as Relief

From MCC's earliest years, one fundamental meaning of service within MCC has been service as discipleship—and, more specifically, service as a lived response to Jesus' command to his disciples in the gospel of Matthew to give food to the hungry and water to the thirsty (Matthew 25:31-46). Service, from this vantage point, is roughly synonymous with relief efforts to meet basic human needs. For many supporters of MCC today, this approach to service shapes their understanding of MCC's mission. Indeed, through the distribution of comforters, relief kits, canned meat, and more, a vital part of MCC service across the decades has been reaching out to the Christ whom we encounter in those who hunger and thirst, with the people who can meat, pack school kits, and fill relief buckets participating in that service effort. Whether responding to famine devastating Mennonite communities in southern Russia through the operation of relief kitchens serving porridge in the early 1920s or distributing food aid and other resources to displaced peoples in

Europe following World War II or shipping MCC canned meat to North Korea or providing relief buckets, comforters, and food parcels to hundreds of thousands of Syrians displaced by the civil war today, a fundamental way that MCC has understood service in the name of Christ over the past century is as a response to Christ's call to meet the basic human needs of neighbors near and far, including the neighbors that citizens of Canada and the U.S. often view as enemies.

MCC administrator Harry Martens captured this understanding of service in the early 1950s in his description of the Pax program in which young men distributed relief supplies and undertook post-war reconstruction in post-World War II Europe. "[Our] aim," he wrote, "is to alleviate human need and tension, give encouragement to the less fortunate in underdeveloped areas of the world or help resettle and rehabilitate the displaced persons in various parts of the world."[1]

Service as Active Nonresistance, an Alternative to War, and a Peace Witness

Much of MCC's work during its first decades unfolded during or in the wake of world wars, with MCC functioning as a channel for the idealism of Mennonite youth who sought to make a contribution to the global good parallel to the self-sacrificial actions of soldiers who had fought and died for their country. In his service application, Clayton Kratz, who participated in the initial MCC relief mission in the 1920s into southern Russia and who would then disappear, presumed dead, wrote in his service application that he wanted to help people in need "because this great world catastrophe [of World War I] has not caused me any inconvenience."[2] Young Mennonites like Kratz sought to be inconvenienced, to sacrifice like other young men of their generation had sacrificed (fig. 21).

---

[1]   Martens, "You Are My Witnesses," undated, 1, in folder Docuware/Publications 1944-Ongoing/News Notes, News Service, News Releases 1944-Ongoing/1953 to 12, scanned from Microfilm Weekly News Notes, pages 172-175, MCC U.S. archives, Akron, Pennsylvania.

[2] Robert Kreider and Rachel Waltner Goossen, *Hungry, Thirsty, a Stranger: The MCC Experience* (Scottdale, PA: Herald Press, 1988), 25.

Fig. 21: In 1920, Clayton Kratz, MCC representative in Russia, stands in front of one of many thousands of horses that died due to lack of feed. Kratz was a member of the first Mennonite unit sent by MCC to initiate relief work. During his assignment, Kratz disappeared (most likely after being taken prisoner by the Red Army) and was never seen again. (MCC photo)

This ideal of self-sacrificial service was understood by many MCC workers as peace work, an active testing and embodiment of the Mennonite conviction of nonresistance, grounded in Jesus' call to his disciples to not resist evil, but instead to return evil with good. The Mennonite doctrine of nonresistance shifted from being the theological basis for separation from the world into a spur for vigorous engagement with it, for demonstrating the power of active Christian love. An MCC document from the mid-1940s, entitled "The Why of Relief Work," portrayed relief service during and after wartime as a form of "real peace work." Such service, wrote the author, "is a particular duty and privilege in time of war, when human sin and destructiveness are doing their worst. To build where others destroy, to heal where others kill, to love when all men hate, is 'to heap coals of fire upon the head' and to overcome evil with good. There is no greater force in the world than the power of Christian love in action. Relief work is a living and powerful testimony to this love at a time when it is most needed."[3]

Civilian Public Service (CPS) workers, conscripted into CPS as an alternative to military service, often connected relief service with Jesus' command to go the second mile, with relief service embodying the principle of overcoming evil with good.[4] To be sure, many CPS men viewed their service as an unwelcome imposition by the government. One anonymous CPS participant observed that "To say that the men in CPS are going the second mile and overcoming evil with good is to look at the picture through rose-colored glasses."[5] Abraham Graber, an Amishman who served in CPS, also observed that "It has been stated that men in CPS are only going the first mile and that often grudgingly. That is far too true," he granted, but he then continued by insisting that "we can go the second mile. If we were not in CPS where could we better represent the principle of going the second mile? If we cannot go the second mile in CPS, then we are admitting that Christianity is not practical in every occasion."[6] CPS participant Marvin Hein reflected back on CPS

---

[3] "The Why of Relief Work," IX-06-03, Box 3, Folder 2/39, "Mennonite Central Committee C.P.S. and other Correspondence 1940-45," File 2 Horst J L 1940, MCC U.S. archives, Akron, Pennsylvania.

[4] For historical accounts and analysis of CPS, see Melvin Gingerich, *Service for Peace: A History of Mennonite Civilian Public Service* (Akron, PA: Mennonite Central Committee, 1949); Mulford Quickert Sibley and Philip E. Jacob, *Conscription of Conscience: The American State and the Conscientious Objector, 1940-1947* (Ithaca, NY: Cornell University Press, 1952); Albert Keim, *The CPS Story: An Illustrated History of Civilian Public Service* (Intercourse, PA: Good Books, 1990); Albert Keim and Grant Stoltzfus, *The Politics of Conscience: The Historic Peace Churches and America at War, 1917-1955* (Scottdale, PA: Herald Press, 1988); Jeffrey Kovac, *Refusing War, Affirming Peace: A History of Civilian Public Service Camp #21 at Cascade Locks* (Corvallis: Oregon State University Press, 2009); Nicholas A. Krehbiel, *General Lewis B. Hershey and Conscientious Objection during World War II* (Columbia: University of Missouri Press, 2011); and Mark Matthews, *Smoke Jumping on the Western Fire Line: Conscientious Objection During World War II* (Norman: University of Oklahoma Press, 2006). See also the Civilian Public Service website: https://civilianpublicservice.org/, accessed August 26, 2020.

[5] Quoted in "Keeping the Vision Clear," *Mennonite CPS Bulletin* 4, no. 9 (November 8, 1945), in folder Docuware/Publications 1944-ongoing/Newsletters/Civilian Public Service newsletter 1942-1947/1945-01-08 to 1945-11-08 CPS Newsletter OCR, MCC U.S. archives, Akron, Pennsylvania.

[6] Abraham Graber, "The CPS Vision," *Mennonite CPS Bulletin* 3, no. 24 (June

as an education in the meaning of Christian service. "Most of us entered CPS largely because we had little choice. We exited CPS persuaded that a life of voluntary Christ-followership demands constant service to other people. For two years we had served our national government, the church and each other. Somehow the conviction that our lives were not our own was translated into an unshakable belief that we were destined as God's people to serve the world."[7]

A decade later, MCC leader Peter Dyck described MCC Pax workers in post-war Europe as "Christian pacifist worker[s] for others in the name of Christ," who forget "self, thinking only of others," who are animated by a "spiritual motivation," and who build "bridges of understanding and goodwill between peoples and communions not by lecturing or preaching but through practical demonstration, through hard physical labor."[8] MCC worker Dorothy Swartzendruber expressed optimism in the power of love-filled service. "Those of us who served on the foreign field know the effects of a love-permeated service," she observed. "In our contacts with people of other nations, other faiths, other customs . . . the folks whom we served through food and clothing distributions, with the down and out, the bewildered refugees, the old people, helpless victims of a cruel war. . . . it was obvious whether or not we were motivated by love."[9] Service as a form of peacebuilding, for Pax man Roy Kauffman, was incarnational, with Pax workers embodying God's love and peace in their lives. "Pax is not merely another movement or demonstration for peace," insisted Kauffman. "Pax men are living examples for peace, demonstrating the love of

---

22, 1945), in folder Docuware/Publications 1944-ongoing/Newsletters/Civilian Public Service newsletter 1942-1947/1945-01-08 to 1945-11-08 CPS Newsletter OCR, MCC U.S. archives, Akron, Pennsylvania.

[7] Marvin Hein, *A Community is Born: The Story of the Birth, Growth, Death and Legacy of Civilian Public Service Camp #138-1, Lincoln, Nebraska 1944-1947* (self-published, 1998), 111-112.

[8] Peter Dyck, "Pax Bridge Builders," *Euro Pax News.* 6, no. 3 (August 1954): 2-3, IX-12-02, Box 4, Folder 4, Euro Pax News, 1954-1959, MCC U.S. archives, Akron, Pennsylvania.

[9] Quoted in Lucille Marr, *The Transforming Power of a Century: Mennonite Central Committee and Its Evolution in Ontario* (Kitchener, ON: Pandora Press, 2003), 100.

God in heart and life."[10] Meanwhile, John Suderman, a Pax man in Bielefeld, Germany, cautioned that the peace witness of service "does not work immediately and there is no promise that there will be no wars; but the Cross indicates that love is rather suffering, than victorious."[11]

Fig. 22: In 1955, Pax men finish construction on one of several housing units in Backnang, Germany, for more than 100 displaced Mennonite families. (MCC photo)

Recognizing that young men entered Pax as an alternative to required military service, Pax administrators sought to foster a spirit of willing self-sacrifice among Pax men (fig. 22).[12] Pax men "are not 'drafted Christians' but rather 'willing second-milers,'" a Pax operations manual stressed.[13] Robert Beyeler, a Pax man in Enkenbach, Germany, told his supervisor that he and other MCC workers faced challenging questions from Europeans about

---

[10] Roy Kauffman, "Pax Men as Peacemakers," *Euro Pax News* 6, no. 2 (May 1959): 2-3, IX-12-02, Box 4, Folder 4, Euro Pax News 1954-1959, MCC U.S. archives, Akron, Pennsylvania.

[11] Quoted in "Minutes of the Pax Peace Conference," Backnang, Germany, August 13-14, 1955, 2, IX-12-02, Box 4, Folder 5, European Pax Peace Conference, MCC U.S. archives, Akron, Pennsylvania.

[12] For an historical overview of the Pax program, see Calvin W. Redekop, *The Pax Story: Service in the Name of Christ, 1951-1976* (Kitchener, ON: Pandora Press, 2001).

[13] Cal Redekop, "Pax Operation Suggestions," November 29, 1952, IX-19-05, Box 6, Folder 5/3, EURO-PAX NEWS Luebeck Unit 1950-1960, MCC U.S. archives, Akron, Pennsylvania.

Fig. 23: Women's Summer Service Unit from Civilian Public Service (CPS) Camp No. 85. at Rhode Island State Hospital for Mental Diseases in Howard, Rhode Island. The unit was one of 26 CPS mental health units operated by MCC, opened in 1943 and closed in 1946. Exact date unknown. (MCC photo)

what motivated their service: "Do you do it because your government requests this from you, or perhaps to see the other side of the world, or are you here to really serve Christ and feel that Pax is a tool used for this purpose?" Beyeler expressed the hope that all Pax men could say that their service was carried out in a spirit of Christian love.[14]

Women in Service

Service through MCC also provided Mennonite women avenues for fulfilling this idealistic desire to demonstrate the power of active Christian love as well as a desire for adventure (fig. 23).[15] Just as the war effort mobilized many women into the work force, so, too, did women become part of the CPS effort. Wives and girlfriends often moved to be based near and work at or close by the camps where their husbands and boyfriends were

---

[14] Robert Beyeler to Robert Good, May 28, 1960, Enkenbach, IX-06-03, Box 174, Folder 101/51, MCC Corresp. 1960 European Pax Services Activity Reports, MCC U.S. archives, Akron, PA.

[15] For an examination of women in service within MCC, see Beth Graybill, "Writing Women into MCC's History," in *A Table of Sharing: Mennonite Central Committee and the Expanding Networks of Mennonite Identity*, ed. Alain Epp Weaver (Telford, PA: Cascadia, 2010), 239-262.

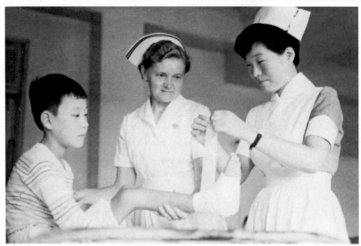

Fig. 24: MCC nurse Tina Letkeman (center), from Graysville, Manitoba, gives instructions to a student nurse at the Presbyterian Hospital in Taegu, Korea, in 1959. (MCC photo)

stationed. Some women served in the camps as nurses. Women's sewing societies prepared "camp kits" to send to CPS that included bedding, towels, toiletries, stationery, and stamps. Over the course of CPS's operations, around 2,000 pacifist women lived in or near the 151 camps, with CPS even operating women's units at eight state-run mental institutions.[16]

Historian Lucille Marr found that "by 1950, forty percent of all MCC overseas workers were single women, nearly double the number of unattached men."[17] Lydia Schlabach, who worked with MCC as a nurse in Korea in the 1950s, described her assignment as "Some glamour, some broadening of experience, some new learning, and a lot of dedication and hard work."[18] (fig. 24) Some women spoke with pride about the connections they forged and the contributions they made in foreign cultures. Lois Martin, who served with Pax in Greece in the 1950s, lifted up the work of MCC women in service, comparing it favorably

---

[16] See Rachel Waltner Goossen, *Women Against the Good War: Conscientious Objection and Gender on the American Homefront, 1941-1947* (Chapel Hill: University of North Carolina Press, 1997), along with the articles in the special issue of MCC's *Women's Concerns Report*, no. 116 (Sept.-Oct. 1994).

[17] Lucille Marr, *Transforming a Century*, 99.

[18] "Girls Who Do What Fellows Couldn't," *Youth's Christian Companion* (September 16, 1962), 13.

to the work of Pax men: "Our fellows do wonderful work on construction of new houses, but haven't you heard of the MCC girls who help village girls construct and mend their clothing?" she asked. "Pax farmers help village farmers mix feeds and make silos, while lady Paxers acquaint village housewives with new recipes," she continued. "As men discuss personal problems with men, so women discuss personal concerns with the women."[19]

Even as the Civilian Public Service, Voluntary Service, Pax, and Teachers Abroad Programs offered new vistas of global engagement by Mennonite women, service expectations and possibilities were significantly shaped by gender norms. "My work must be congenial, my words pleasant and kind and I must contribute my share toward a smooth and effective unit," explained Tina Warkentin, a so-called Pax matron in Panyasita, Greece, who cooked, cleaned, and mended clothing for Pax "boys." "Always I must place Christ, others, and the work before self."[20] To be sure, Pax men were also expected to live lives of self-sacrifice, but when applied to MCC women in service, the call to self-denial also reinforced a gendered hierarchy. Sometimes Pax matrons chafed at these norms, expressing the type of discontent that Betty Friedan would capture in *The Feminine Mystique* about the expectation that women would find fulfillment in housework. Reflecting on a long day of cooking and cleaning for the Pax men, Anne Driedger, Pax matron in Bechterdissen near Bielefeld, Germany, confessed "I do not feel satisfied and can't help wondering: is there really a purpose to my being here? [I]s making meals and scrubbing floors my sole purpose for being here?" Continuing her musings, Driedger concluded that she could find meaning in the housework by viewing it not as "wasted time and effort" but rather as a contribution to the church's witness that "the wrong in the world can never be made right by force and bloodshed" and to

---

[19] Ibid.

[20] Tina Warkentin, "Experiences and Observations in Greece," 2, Information Service (News Service), October 17, 1958, MCC U.S. archives, Akron, Pennsylvania.

"a Savior who teaches us to love all men and do good unto them."[21] (fig. 25)

Fig. 25: Pax matron Anne Driedger, of Winnipeg, Manitoba, is amused as Pax man Elwin LeFevre, of Sterling, Illinois, looks to see what is cooking. LeFevre was unit leader and Driedger was matron at the Pax house in Bechterdissen, near Bielefeld, Germany, where Pax men were helping to build houses for refugee families in 1955. (MCC photo)

Service as Patriotic Duty

Even as MCC service was understood as the active witness of nonresistant love in action, service during MCC's first half-century also represented an alternative form of service to one's country. Through MCC's Civilian Public Service, Pax, and Teachers Abroad Programs, Mennonites from the United States fulfilled a patriotic obligation by contributing to the imagined good of their country. So, for example, MCC's executive committee declared in a September 1943 statement that the Mennonite men in Civilian Public Service who fought fires, worked in mental hospitals, and carried out forestry and soil conservation activities were fulfilling a patriotic duty: CPS service, the board insisted, "has meaning to the men who

---

[21] Anne Driedger, "This is Not a Dream!" *European Relief Notes* (January-February 1956), 8, in folder Docuware/Publications 1944-ongoing/Relief Notes 1920-/European Relief Notes/European Relief Notes 1956 Vol 12 No 01 January February and March, MCC U.S. archives, Akron, Pennsylvania.

perform it as an expression of loyalty and love to their country, and of their desire to make a contribution to its welfare."[22] (fig. 26) A decade later in 1954, Omar Lapp, a Pax man in Backnang, Germany, described his MCC service as patriotic action: "To be a patriot," Lapp explained, "means to contribute the best we can to the welfare of our nation and this is our active peace position rather than taking up arms."[23]

As the Cold War then began to take shape in the 1950s, some in MCC's Pax program presented Mennonite relief, reconstruction, and rehabilitation efforts in post-World War II Europe as contributing to the anti-communist cause. The Pax program, contended MCC administrator Harry Martens, "serves as a rebuke to those who are saying the Christian church does not care for a brother in need. This is a rebuke to communism

Fig. 26: Civilian Public Service workers help clear fallen trees after a March 1942 tornado in Lacon, Illinois. From left, Floyd F. Yoder from Kalona, Iowa, Orville C. Smith from Sumner, Iowa, and three other men (names unknown). (MCC photo)

---

[22] 1943 MCC board statement about CPS, in folder Docuware/Binational (BN) Minutes & Meeting Packets 1920 to 2012, Annual Meeting of the Mennonite Central Committee #110, December 30-31, 1943, MCC U.S. archives, Akron, Pennsylvania.

[23] Omar Lapp, "Minutes of the Pax Peace Conference," 2, Backnang, Germany, August 13-14, 1955, IX-12-02, Box 4, Folder 5, European Pax Peace Conference, MCC U.S. archives, Akron, Pennsylvania.

that seems to find its way in where the Christian Church has failed to do its part."[24] Reflecting on the Pax unit in northern Greece, MCC worker Dwight Wiebe claimed that an "important objective" of MCC's service program in Greece was "the demonstration of our Peace Witness in an area of international tension." The "small mountain villages" where Pax agricultural extension workers lived and worked, Wiebe explained, "have always been a breeding ground and a no-man's land for factions participating in the civil war. . . . The need for removing the causes of Communism is one of the greatest challenges confronting Christianity today. Removing the causes for war presents a great opportunity for our Peace witness."[25] (fig. 27)

Fig. 27: Pax man J. Lester Yoder, of Belleville, Pennsylvania, with a Greek farmer discussing an MCC hog husbandry program in 1962. (MCC photo/Vernon Cross)

To be sure, not all MCC workers understood their service as the fulfillment of a patriotic duty or as the reinforcement of the Western world's battle against communism. An appeal for volunteers in the *Canadian Mennonite* in 1955, for example, viewed MCC's Voluntary Service program as "the answer to the

[24] Harry Martens, "You Are My Witnesses," 2.
[25] Dwight Wiebe, "Status of Pax Greece 1955," 1, 1955-07-16 #229 Executive Committee minutes, MCC U.S. archives, Akron Pennsylvania.

materialism and militarism of our day."[26] For Paxman Jim Juhnke, Pax service expressed allegiance to God above country. "As a Christian I pledge prime allegiance to God," Juhnke stressed, "not to the flag of the United States of America, not to the St. Louis Cardinal baseball team, and not to Colgate toothpaste." Such obedience, he continued, demanded nonresistant discipleship, which Juhnke defined as "complete obedience to God's will." Nonresistance, he stressed, was not "passive" or "negative," but rather an active "outgoing of love and service to fellow men."[27] Allegiance to God, for Juhnke, not only stood higher than allegiance to country: allegiance to a militarized United States actively conflicted with allegiance to God. "We speak glibly of the love of God" in the United States, wrote Juhnke. "We print, 'In God we trust' on our coins. But we don't trust God. We trust machine guns, ballistic missiles and H bombs. We trust in the $40 billion we give each year for defense. We believe that if it weren't for our armies, evil forces would overtake major portions of the world. So we pay our taxes and hide behind the flimsy protection they can buy." For Juhnke, then, MCC service thus represented not so much an alternative form of patriotic duty but rather an alternative to idolatrous militarism. "I am a Paxman because I believe that Christ was telling the truth when he proposed that loving your enemies and blessing them that curse you was the way of God," Juhnke confessed. "I believe that the love of Christ is practical. Not only can this love work miracles within the heart of an individual. It is the answer to suspicion, fear and mistrust which usually ends in violence."[28] (fig. 28)

---

[26] *The Canadian Mennonite* (January 28, 1955), quoted in Marr, *The Transforming Power of a Century*, 110.

[27] Jim Juhnke, "What Nonresistance Means to Me?" February 21, 1959, IX-19-05, Box 7, Folder 5/19, EURO-PAX NEWS PAX Men Statements 1950-1960, MCC U.S. archives, Akron, Pennsylvania.

[28] Jim Juhnke, "A Paxer's Testimony," received May 11, 1959, 1-2, IX-12-02, Box 4, Folder 7, European Pax Services, MCC U.S. archives, Akron, Pennsylvania.

Fig. 28: Pax volunteers (from left) Ken Von Gunten of Berne, Indiana, Stanley Gerber of Walnut Creek, Ohio, Gordon Walters of Etna Green, Indiana, Ken Hershey of Bird-in-Hand, Pennsylvania, Herman Zuercher of Wooster, Ohio, and Robert Beyeler of Wooster, Ohio, with their mopeds in Germany in 1960. Some of the mopeds had as many as five or six Pax owners and were handed down from Pax man to Pax man. (MCC photo/Jim Juhnke)

Service versus Witness?

Over the decades, MCC leaders have underscored that MCC service assignments represented a form of proactive Christian witness. So, for example, MCC leaders in Canada in 1955 described MCC's Voluntary Service program as an "avenue of a thorough and lasting witness of God's love for man in a hardened and indifferent society."[29] Around the same time, Pax administrators stated that one of the program's purposes was "to provide an opportunity for a positive Christian witness by the individual and the unit."[30] Through MCC service, an MCC administrator observed, "our young people have found unusual opportunities for a Christian witness to our Lord and Saviour," as Pax men sought "to witness for peace as found in Jesus Christ

---

[29] *The Canadian Mennonite* (January 28, 1955), quoted in Marr, *The Transforming Power of a Century*, 110.

[30] "A Day in Pax," 11, 1965, script for filmstrip, IX-26-05, Box 1, MCC U.S. archives, Akron, Pennsylvania.

and as he taught us through brotherly love."[31] One popular form of witness in the Pax program was singing: choruses of Pax participants traveled around post-war Europe to share the good news through singing in churches, refugee camps, and prisons.[32]

Even as MCC leaders described its service programs as a form of witness, some of MCC's supporting churches became concerned that MCC service was becoming decoupled from evangelistic witness. Responding to these concerns, MCC convened a consultation in 1958 attended by representatives from several Mennonite churches and church agencies. At the consultation, Brethren in Christ leader and chair of the MCC board, C.N. Hostetter, granted that there was a "danger of an overemphasis on purely social service," adding that it was important that MCC's "relief ministry 'In the Name of Christ' be more than a nominal cliché," concluding that "unless our workers know Christ, give themselves to Christ as they give themselves for others and witness positively for Christ, our program falls short as Christian relief."[33]

This concern about the potential separation of "word and deed" has surfaced repeatedly over the ensuing decades from multiple directions, with different Anabaptist churches worried about what they perceived as MCC's lack of verbal witness to the gospel. In this book's final chapter, I examine understandings of Christian mission in tension within MCC, offering one perspective on how word and deed have come together in MCC service over the decades.

Service as Transformative Education

Even as service in MCC's early decades was viewed as a one-way response of discipleship from the U.S. and Canada to the rest of the world, narratives within MCC complicated this unidirectional picture. MCC leaders Robert Kreider and Ron

---

[31] Martens, "You Are My Witnesses," 1.

[32] "Building Bridges" (no author, no date), IX-19-05, Box 7, Folder 5/10, EURO-PAX NEWS Articles 1950-1960, MCC U.S. archives, Akron, Pennsylvania.

[33] Quoted in "Minutes of the Study Meeting on the Relationship of MCC Relief and Service Programs and Mennonite Missions," held at Mennonite Home Mission, Chicago, IL, January 24, 1958, in folder Docuware/Binational (BN) Minutes & Meeting Packets 1920 to 2012, MCC U.S. archives, Akron, Pennsylvania.

Mathies described MCC service as "continuing education" and "transformative education," highlighting that the life-long impact on those who went out in service was as great if not greater than the impact their service had had on others.[34] One MCC administrator highlighted the educational character of MCC service, observing that MCC "workers who have spent two or more years working in an area of need and with a people in a different land and culture will not return the same as they went. To many of them this is a school of 'hard knocks.' They are away from comfortable homes, a land of plenty and now living under very modest circumstances and day after day see human need and despair."[35] Canadian Brethren in Christ leader E.J. Swalm also called attention to the transformative impact of MCC service: "Surely we have noticed that many of them have forever had their pattern of life change. Once they have responded to a term of gratuitous service whether at home or abroad they never seem quite contented to do anything else."[36] The editor of the Mennonite Church publication, *Youth's Christian Service*, made the same point in a slightly tongue-in-cheek manner, writing that "Mr. Paxman returns home with a hatred for materialism and a passion for peace and social action. He feels he has a gleam of truth that daren't be lost, and he will try to put it across every chance he gets."[37] (fig. 29)

Service as Listening, Waiting, and Presence

The 1970s saw the start of a multi-decade creative ferment and rethinking within MCC about the nature of service. In 1976, for example, Urbane Peachey, then MCC's Peace Section executive secretary and Middle East director, penned a provocative article

---

[34] See Robert Kreider, "The Impact of MCC Service on American Mennonites," *Mennonite Quarterly Review* 44, no. 3 (July 1970): 245-261 and Ronald J.R. Mathies, "Service as (Trans)formation: MCC as Educational Institution," in *Unity amidst Diversity: Mennonite Central Committee at 75* (Akron, PA: MCC, 1996), 69-81.

[35] Harry Martens, "You Are My Witnesses," 2-3.

[36] E.J. Swalm, "The Church Contributing to the Transformation of Society: Reading from I Cor. 16:8-21 and I Cor. 9:12," 3, MCC Canada minutes, January 13-14, 1967, Minutes #18, Annual Meeting held at Elmwood Mennonite Brethren Church, Winnipeg, Manitoba, MCC U.S. archives, Akron, Pennsylvania.

[37] Editor, "Paxman Come Home," *Youth's Christian Companion* (September 16, 1962): 30.

Fig. 29: Pax man Kenneth Erb of Casselton, North Dakota, poses with a home-built forage chopper in Bolivia in 1968. For the equivalent of US$10, he built the chopper from an assortment of used items, including cultivator beams, barrels, and broken truck springs. (MCC photo)

for MCC's internal publication, *Intercom*, entitled "Service—Who Needs It?" "We've really done our best to send skilled personnel who could make a needed contribution," Peachey wrote, "but now there are a number of countries which are interested in our aid but not our personnel." MCC should ask itself: "Who is asking for the relationship? With whose needs are we primarily concerned?" Was MCC concerned with the need of Anabaptists from Canada and the U.S. to serve, or with the self-identified priorities of churches and communities in the countries where MCC operated (which might not include the placement of workers from the U.S. and Canada)?[38]

Such questions about what role, if any, service workers from Canada and the U.S. might fruitfully play internationally became more pressing as countries around the world gained greater independence from former colonial powers and with the rise of a professional class and the growth and development of civil society organizations in those countries. These types of questions also gained in intensity as MCC moved from direct

[38] Urbane Peachey, "Service—Who Needs It?" *Intercom* 16, no. 4 (April 1976): 5-6.

implementation of program to greater partnership with and accompaniment of local churches and civil society organizations.

Beginning in the mid-1970s, service started to be redefined as learning. Responding to Peachey's 1976 *Intercom* article, Atlee Beechy, a member of MCC's executive committee, wondered if "perhaps it is time to redefine the meaning of service, to recognize more fully the two-way dimension of service, including the notion that learning from others is an act of service."[39] Such pondering was accompanied by active debates within MCC over the following decades about colonial and racialized assumptions about who is serving whom and where,

Fig. 30: MCC worker Pauline Sawatzky (back, right), from Pawnee Rock, Kansas, is pictured with co-workers at the Southern Christian Leadership Conference office in Atlanta, Georgia, in 1962. (MCC photo)

with some visions of service critiqued for their implicit understanding of service as a unidirectional initiative of white Mennonites of European heritage to the rest of the world. Reflecting back on these debates in the late 1990s, Judy

---

[39] Atlee Beechy, "Who Needs Service?" *Intercom* 16, no. 5 (May 1976): 3.

Zimmerman Herr summarized these concerns in the form of questions: "Does being in a giving posture demean those we send our help to? . . . Is our service really an expression of power? How do we prevent our service from becoming an attitude of self-righteousness?"[40] As MCC workers in service assignments in places like Atlanta, New Orleans, and Gulfport, Mississippi, encountered the stark reality of racism in the United States, they also began to highlight MCC's organizational whiteness and the racialized character of MCC's global service, with predominantly white Mennonites from Canada and the U.S. going out to the primarily black and brown countries of the global South (fig. 30).

Probing questions about service and power in the seventies and eighties led to a redefinition within MCC of service as learning and presence. So, for example, Bertha Beachy, a long-time Mennonite worker in Somalia, wrote in 1978 that Christian service workers needed to adopt the stance of being "eternal learners" and to participate in "the rhythm of people's lives."[41] The redefinition of service as learning was crystallized in a 1986 review of MCC Africa's work led by Tim Lind. "Africans have suffered under centuries of words and theories of change/development coming from the North," Lind observed. "It is in this context that servanthood for us today means abandoning all of the good and useful things we have to say in Africa in favor of a listening stance." MCC workers from Canada and the U.S., Lind argued, needed to take a "back seat" and adopt a "waiting" posture. Revisioning service as listening and learning, Lind recognized, "may seem to some less than exciting and creative, particularly as it involves a shift in our thinking about ourselves as initiators and planners of activities and responses to need. However," he continued, "we feel that this posture is in fact highly creative as it allows space and visibility to approaches to service and development which are different

---

[40] Judy Zimmerman Herr, "Service as Incarnation," 1998, 3, IX-60 1998 Box 14 Folder title: PI Service as Incarnation, MCC U.S. archives, Akron, Pennsylvania.

[41] Bertha Beachy, "Culture Shock in an Islamic Society," IX-12-7, MCC TAP Orientation, Akron, PA (August 19, 1978), MCC archives, Akron, Pennsylvania.

from our Western approaches, and which can mix with our own approaches in new and exciting ways."[42]

This reconceptualization in the seventies and eighties of service as a multidirectional movement of listening, learning, and sharing has shaped MCC service programs up to the present. This new understanding of service was reflected in the name adopted by MCC when it inaugurated an eleven-month service program in the early 1980s for young adults from Canada and the U.S. to the rest of the world: Serving and Learning Together (SALT). In later years, the Serving with Appalachian Peoples (SWAP) program, operated by MCC in Kentucky and West Virginia, changed its name to Sharing with Appalachian Peoples. Jean Snyder, an MCC worker in Jamaica in the mid-1980s, emphasized that without a learning stance, service work threatened to devolve into pointless activity: "Unless we learn from the people themselves . . . who they are and why they see themselves, the world, us and God as they do, we have little to offer them but our busyness," she explained. "And our busyness may, in the long run, have more relevance to our monthly reports than to the lives we touch."[43]

The heightened stress on service as learning generated intense self-reflection and soul-searching on the part of MCC service workers, captured regularly in free-form quarterly reports to MCC administrators, with some reflections shared within MCC's internal staff publication, *Intercom*, which ran from the early 1960s into the mid-1990s. "Show us our poverty of spirit and the leanness of our souls," offered Judith Dick, an MCC human rights worker in the Occupied West Bank in 1987, in a prayer published in *Intercom*. "Teach us to untangle our hearts and to love with a love like yours/Expose the prejudices and injustices in our own thought and actions."[44] Self-reflection sometimes became self-criticism about perceived failures or inabilities to

---

[42] Tim Lind, "Inquiry into MCC Africa Purpose and Presence," paper for the MCC board of directors meeting, September 1986, 1-2, in folder Docuware/Africa 1960-ongoing/1986 Roll #77/02 Africa Data through Africa Peace Tour-Peace Committee (AF), MCC U.S. archives, Akron, Pennsylvania.

[43] Jean Snyder, "Learning about Culture in Jamaica," *Intercom* 30, no. 6 (July-August 1986): 2.

[44] Judith Dick, "Prayer," *Intercom* 31, no. 5 (May 1987): 1.

become fully immersed in a new cultural setting. "I've been a tourist for four years," lamented Hilda Kurtz, an agricultural development worker in Kenya the late 1980s. "I want to live life, not watch it. I will always be a tourist here. I am weary of the role."[45] Karen Kanagy, who served as an MCC community development worker in Bolivia in the mid-1980s, shared this lament. "I know that some of my actions, attitudes and possessions created walls and barriers [between me and my Bolivian neighbors] that kept us from truly understanding each other," Kanagy wrote upon completing her service term. "I allowed my North American self to get in the way of forming more intimate relationships with Bolivians and because of that I was unable to be a more powerful witness to God's love. It also kept me from discovering the possibility of who I could truly be in the Bolivian setting. I was sensitive, loving and understanding to a point. I went the first mile. But the second? How much did I allow God and the people around me to determine my identity in Bolivia?"[46]

The past four decades or so have witnessed an expansion in MCC's understanding of who is engaged in service and where and a redefinition of service as a sharing of gifts that *builds* on the *strengths* of local communities rather than focusing on *helping* them in their *need*. MCC U.S.'s Summer Service program, for example, has provided opportunities for young adults of color since 1983 to serve in their local communities. Meanwhile, beginning in 2004 and continuing up to the present, the Young Anabaptist Mennonite Exchange Network (YAMEN) has operated in partnership with Mennonite World Conference, offering eleven-month service opportunities for young adults outside of Canada and the U.S. to other parts of the Majority World, opportunities through which the global church shares gifts of service with one another. The International Volunteer Exchange Program (IVEP), initially established in 1950 to

---

[45] Hilda Kurtz, "A Lament," *Intercom* 33, no. 2 (February 1989): 4.
[46] Karen Kanagy, "Reflections of a Returned MCCer," *Intercom* 30, no. 4 (May 1986): 3.

Fig. 31: Danitza Padilla, a 2007-2008 participant in MCC's International Volunteer Exchange Program (IVEP) from Bolivia, works on a quilt in the West Coast MCC Quilting Center in Reedley, California, in 2008.(MCC photo/Kathy Heinrichs Wiest)

provide European Mennonites with one-year service opportunities in the United States and Canada, now includes participants from over 25 countries (fig. 31). Meanwhile, an increasing percentage of MCC's multi-year workers, including program administrators, come from outside Canada and the United States.

The broader contexts within which MCC service takes place are ever evolving. The number of young adults in MCC's south-south exchange program, YAMEN, has almost doubled over the past five years, while the number of young adults from Canada and the U.S. participating in the one-year SALT program has dropped by about 20% in this same period (fig. 32). Increased restrictions on visas by many countries, including Canada and the U.S., present barriers to MCC's intercultural service programs, barriers reinforced by government regulations responding to the global COVID-19 pandemic. Organizations receiving expatriate MCC service workers have greater expectations of those workers bringing professional and even specialized skills. MCC's short-term SALT program of eleven months appears to many prospective candidates as demanding a long-term commitment. Young adults in the United States today come out of university education with unprecedented levels of student debt, and understandably seek service assignments that will fit within a career trajectory. The landscapes of Christian service are in dramatic flux. A key challenge for MCC, as an organization committed to "service in the name of Christ," will thus be discerning how to navigate this shifting landscape at the dawn of its second century.

Fig. 32: Young Anabaptist Mennonite Exchange Network (YAMEN) participant Godswill Muzarabani of Zimbabwe teaches English in Lao People's Democratic Republic in 2012. (MCC photo/Silas Crews)

Chapter 4: First to the Household of Faith? MCC, Humanitarianism, and the Church

In his letter to the Galatian church, the Apostle Paul exhorts his readers to "not grow weary in doing what is right, for we will reap at harvest-time, if we do not give up. So then, whenever we have an opportunity, let us work for the good of all, and especially for those of the family of faith." (Galatians 6:9-10, NRSV). Paul calls Christ's followers to live lives conformed to and shaped by God's Spirit, lives marked by doing good for all, with an emphasis on doing good to those within what Paul names the *family* or *household* of faith. MCC leaders repeatedly cited the phrase, "especially unto them who are of the household of faith" (KJV), during MCC's first decades as they described MCC's mandate. The creation of MCC in the early 1920s to respond to famine in southern Russia did not emerge from a generalized humanitarian impulse, but rather from an appeal from *Glaubensgenossen,* or relatives in the faith, an appeal from Mennonites for assistance as they faced acute hunger. For some of the Mennonite groups that came together to form MCC, the *Glaubensgenossen* who appealed for assistance were not only relatives in the faith, but also near and distant family members. MCC's next major initiatives in the 1930s and during World War II also responded to needs within the Mennonite "household of faith": first, in the late twenties and early thirties, with MCC arranging for and assisting in the settlement of Mennonite refugees from Soviet Russia to the Paraguayan Chaco, and second, the World War II collaboration with Quakers, the Church of the Brethren, and other groups in lobbying for, creating, and administering the Civilian Public Service program that allowed Amish, Brethren in Christ, Mennonite, Mennonite Brethren, and other conscientious objectors to undertake "work of national importance" as an alternative to military service.

One way to narrate MCC's first decades, then, would be to describe MCC as focused on providing assistance to those within the "household of faith," or, as a booklet published by MCC on the occasion of its silver anniversary in 1945 phrased it, "the bringing of relief to stricken members of the Mennonite body."[1]

---

[1] *Twenty-Five Years: 1920-1945* (Akron, PA: Mennonite Central Committee, 1945), 8.

Yet such a recounting of MCC's early decades would be incomplete. Narrating MCC's first years as narrowly focused on the needs of the *Glaubensgenossen* would fail to account for how the 1920s famine response in southern Russia reached non-Mennonites as well as Mennonites. Nor would an account of the Civilian Public Service program as primarily about the need to create alternatives to military service for Mennonite young men adequately capture how CPS pushed Mennonites to care about doing good for all beyond the Mennonite church, with the experience of CPSers in places like Gulfport, Mississippi, and in assignments within mental hospitals sowing the seeds of future Mennonite involvement in efforts for racial justice and in the establishment of mental health care facilities that sought to provide more humane treatment for people with mental illness. What began as doing good to those within the church expanded into broader efforts to do good.

Fig. 33: From left, Mukundi Kabemba, Mulumba Mpay, Talama God (host family member) and Muyaya Tshiepela, with help from Ditutu Omer (in white shirt, member of a local relief committee), feed their pigs at the Kanzala piggery in Tshikapa, Kasai province, Democratic Republic of the Congo. MCC partnered with Communauté Mennonite au Congo (Mennonite Church of Congo) to distribute pigs and piggeries that provide food and income for displaced families living in Tshikapa. (MCC photo/Kambaba Lwamba)

While references within MCC reports, memos, and external news releases to the Galatians 6:10 passage taper off beginning in the 1950s, the tension encapsulated within Paul's admonition to do good for all, especially to those within the household of faith, a tension between the particular and the universal, between doing good to all and doing good to those to whom one is close (one's family, friends, neighbors, and fellow church members), has persisted across MCC's history. For example, when responding to mass displacement that began in the summer of 2016 within the Kasai region of the Democratic Republic of the Congo, MCC asked: should MCC focus its humanitarian assistance exclusively or primarily on the thousands of Mennonites displaced from Kasai (fig. 33)? Or should its response be determined solely by needs-based criteria? What is the role of partnership with Congolese Mennonite churches in carrying out and determining the shape of such a response? These questions are emblematic of a persistent tension not just for MCC, but for Christian relief agencies more broadly, a tension between a theologically-grounded mission of working with, through, and for the church, on the one hand, and a commitment to humanitarian principles such as impartiality, proportionality, and neutrality, on the other. Tension, to be sure, is not the same as fundamental incompatibility or irreconcilable conflict—it does, however, reflect that MCC has sought from its inception to hold together two values that can at times sit uncomfortably within one another, namely, the humanitarian value of impartial assistance based solely on need and the value of providing mutual aid within the church.

This chapter probes how MCC has attempted in its history to hold these potentially conflicting commitments in tension with one another. I begin by providing a brief overview of the development of modern humanitarianism and of the values embedded within contemporary humanitarian standards to which MCC and other church-based relief agencies adhere, noting the suspicions that some humanitarian actors have of religiously-rooted actors engaged in emergency responses to address basic human needs. I then turn to a discussion of how MCC leaders described MCC's humanitarian relief efforts during the organization's first quarter century, examining how they viewed doing good to all and doing good for fellow Mennonites as fundamentally compatible. I next look at correspondence from Mennonite relief workers in post-World War II Europe that shows them both fending off accusations of sectarian preference in relief distribution and objecting to what they viewed as the overly narrow focus of other Christian aid actors on assisting members of their own churches. After the 1950s, MCC references to responding first to the household of faith began to disappear, surfacing only occasionally, as the organization's commitment to the principle of impartiality in the distribution of humanitarian assistance became increasingly embedded within the organization. Yet, as I suggest in the concluding section of this chapter, the decline starting in the 1950s of MCC citations of Paul's admonition to do good especially to the household of faith does not mean that the tension between humanitarian principles and the commitment to working with, through, and for the church disappears. Indeed, I argue that this enduring tension stems in part from the fact that MCC has played two main functions since its inception—not only working to meet basic human needs in the name of Christ, but also functioning as an ecumenical engine that, by bringing together people and churches of divergent faith commitments, has forged ever-shifting and often-expanding understandings of who belongs within the household of faith.

On a Needs-Only Basis: The Principles of Modern Humanitarianism

The modern humanitarian movement begins with the founding of the International Committee of the Red Cross (ICRC) in 1863.[2] The Swiss businessman Henry Dunant, deeply disturbed by the suffering he witnessed in the aftermath of the 1859 Battle of Solferino in Italy, became a leading proponent of the principle that emergency assistance to the wounded and needy should be offered without discrimination. Together with a group of prominent citizens of Geneva, Switzerland, Dunant founded the ICRC to promote a vision of humanitarian action

---

[2] For an analytical history of the ICRC, see Douglas Forsythe, *The Humanitarians: The International Committee of the Red Cross* (Cambridge and New York: Cambridge University Press, 2005). Michael Barnett offers a broader account of humanitarianism in *Empire of Humanity: A History of Humanitarianism* (Ithaca, NY: Cornell University Press, 2013).

during times of war guided by principles of non-discrimination and impartiality and of an international order that enshrined such humanitarian principles. This humanitarian movement born in Switzerland grew rapidly, with the founding over the ensuing decades of scores of national Red Cross and Red Crescent societies. The burgeoning Red Cross movement mobilized during World War I to care for prisoners of war and to provide relief assistance to civilian populations besieged by armed conflict. For its efforts during the war, the ICRC received the Nobel Peace Prize in 1917. Two years later, the International Federation of Red Cross and Red Crescent Societies established a set of fundamental principles that have defined modern humanitarianism over the past century.

One of these foundational humanitarian principles promoted by the Red Cross/Red Crescent movement was impartiality, or non-discrimination, in the provision of humanitarian assistance. When providing aid, the Red Cross/Red Crescent movement stressed, humanitarian actors must make "no discrimination as to nationality, race, religious beliefs, class or political opinions," but must rather be "guided solely by the . . . needs [of suffering individuals]," giving "priority to the most urgent cases of distress." Humanitarian actors must "help people regardless of their religious beliefs, the colour of their skin, their political convictions, where they come from, or whether they are rich or poor," ensuring that "those in greatest need receive assistance first" and making distribution decisions on a "needs only" basis that is "not influenced by personal considerations or feelings."[3]

More recent efforts by today's humanitarian actors, from United Nations agencies to donor governments to international non-governmental organizations such as MCC, to articulate basic humanitarian principles have returned again and again to the fundamental standards first expressed by the Red Cross/Red Crescent. For example, the Sphere Standards, first developed in 1997 as a multi-agency effort to improve the consistency and quality of humanitarian aid, stipulate that humanitarian

---

[3] The ICRC's basic principles can be found here:
https://www.icrc.org/sites/default/files/topic/file_plus_list/4046-the_fundamental_principles_of_the_international_red_cross_and_red_crescent_movement.pdf. Accessed August 23, 2020.

assistance "must be provided according to the principle of impartiality, which requires that it be provided solely on the basis of need and in proportion to need. This reflects the wider principle of non-discrimination: that no one should be discriminated against on any grounds of status, including age, gender, race, colour, ethnicity, sexual orientation, language, religion, disability, health status, political or other opinion, and national or social origin."[4] The Core Humanitarian Standard of 2014, another multi-agency initiative that emerged in part from the Sphere project and which laid out nine commitments for humanitarian agencies to use in measuring and assessing the quality of their actions, underscores that humanitarian agencies must "design and implement appropriate programmes based on an impartial assessment of needs and risks" and "commit to providing impartial assistance based on the needs and capacities of communities and people affected by crisis."[5]

In its efforts to provide food, basic hygiene items, shelter, and other forms of humanitarian aid to individuals and communities devastated by war, earthquakes, hurricanes, tsunamis, volcanic eruptions, and more, MCC, along with other Christian relief agencies such as World Vision and Catholic Relief Services, seeks to adhere to the principles and commitments developed by Sphere and the Core Humanitarian Standard, including the principle of the impartial provision of humanitarian assistance on the basis of need alone, without regard to the religious identity of recipients. Some humanitarian actors, however, express skepticism about the commitment of faith-based organizations like MCC to humanitarian principles. So, for example, an internal study commissioned in 2014 by Lutheran World Relief of senior development professionals working for USAID and international NGOs regarding their perceptions of faith-based organizations found ambivalent attitudes. On the

---

[4] *The Sphere Handbook: Humanitarian Charter and Minimum Standards in Humanitarian Response* (Geneva: Sphere Association, 2018), 30. The *Handbook* is available for download at https://spherestandards.org/handbook/editions/. Accessed August 23, 2020.

[5] See *Core Humanitarian Standard on Quality and Accountability* (London: CHS Alliance, 2014), 10 (points 1.2 and 1.4). The Standard is available for download at https://corehumanitarianstandard.org/the-standard/language-versions. Accessed August 23, 2020.

one hand, respondents generally affirmed faith-based organizations as a positive force in international humanitarian efforts, thanks to their connectedness to local networks and their responsiveness to beneficiaries. At the same time, however, respondents voiced concerns about faith-based humanitarian actors potentially tying their assistance to the religious identity of recipients or to proselytizing activities: such critics worry that Christian, Muslim and other religious humanitarian organizations may compromise humanitarian principles such as impartiality by directing their assistance first to their respective households of faith.[6]

"Entirely Non-Partisan" or "Prior Consideration" for Mennonites?

During MCC's first two decades or so, its leaders saw minimal tension between the humanitarian principle of impartiality and commitment to first responding to those within the household of faith. In the early 1940s, prior to the U.S. entry into the Second World War, MCC chairman Orie O. Miller wrote in a letter to MCC representative in Germany M.C. Lehman that "Our work, as you know, is entirely nonpartisan—relief to be extended without preference as to race, nationality, or otherwise, with particular attention to relief needs among war suffering women and children." Miller continued: "In case, of course, that there should be relief needs among the Mennonite folks of Europe, these should also receive prior consideration . . ." For Miller, being "entirely nonpartisan" and giving "prior consideration" to "the Mennonite folks of Europe" were perfectly congruent.[7]

---

[6] See the introduction by Alain Epp Weaver to the focus issue of *Intersections: MCC Theory and Practice Quarterly* 4, no. 4 (Fall 2016): 1-3, on the topic of "The Difference Faith Makes."

[7] John D. Unruh, *In the Name of Christ: A History of the Mennonite Central Committee* (Scottdale, PA: Herald Press, 1952): 42.

Fig. 34: This feeding center in Trans-Volga, Russia, circa 1922, was one of 140 MCC-supported centers in southern Russia that distributed at least 25,000 rations daily at the peak of the relief efforts. (MCC photo)

MCC came into being as a response to a call for help from within the "household of faith," through the decision of diverse Mennonite churches to collaborate in a joint response to the plea from Mennonites in what was then southern Russia for food assistance in the face of famine (fig. 34). The booklet published by MCC on the occasion of its silver anniversary in 1945 presented the decision to create MCC as a channel for collaborative action as a decision that "spontaneously grew out of the desire of the Mennonite brotherhood to feed the hungry, clothe the naked, and to testify by loving service to the Gospel of peace and love."[8] Not just feed any hungry people, but specifically hungry Mennonites: "There was no wavering in the mind of the brethren who decided to take the step—the brotherhood in Russia was stricken with famine; it was the Christian duty and privilege of the churches in America to bring assistance."[9] In a retrospective summary in 1929 of this first MCC initiative, MCC leaders P.C. Hiebert and Orie Miller described MCC's famine response that ran from 1920 to 1925 in southern Russia as a response to "the sufferings of our brethren"

---

[8] *Twenty-Five Years 1920-1945*, 4
[9] Ibid., 6.

Fig. 35: Tractors sent by Mennonites in the United States arrived in Khortitza in southern Russia in October 1922. (MCC photo)

and as a "common great work of mercy 'to them of the household of faith,' and others."[10] (fig. 35)

The "and others" at the end of this sentence might read as an afterthought: Hiebert and Miller recognized that the readers whom they sought to reach with their book-length summary report on the famine relief effort were primarily interested in how MCC had assisted the Mennonite household of faith. Yet Hiebert and Miller's reference to "and others" also functions as a recognition that the Pauline call to do good "to them of the household of faith" is paired with the more universal call to do good to all people. Miller and Hiebert's report presented MCC's famine response not only as an answer to the appeal from Mennonites in Russia, but also as emerging from the desire of Mennonites in the U.S. and Canada to live out the Mennonite doctrine of nonresistance in an active, not simply negative, manner. Noting that there "was little satisfaction in just maintaining a negative position toward war," Hiebert and Miller described Mennonites in the U.S. and Canada as seeking "an opportunity to disprove the charges of cowardice and selfishness

---

[10] P.C. Hiebert and Orie Miller, *Feeding the Hungry: Russia Famine, 1919-1925* (Scottdale, PA: Mennonite Central Committee, 1929), 222.

made against the conscientious objectors, and to express in a positive, concrete way the principles of peace and good-will in which they believed." The call for help from Russia offered the chance to express Mennonite peace convictions in a positive way: "The need there was great, little was being done, and there was the added incentive of being able to help and to work with and through those of our own household of faith."[11]

MCC's famine relief response in southern Russia in the early 1920s can from one perspective be viewed as a new variation on a longer history of mutual aid within and between Anabaptist groups, a history that can be traced back to the Dutch Mennonite *Fonds voor buitenlandsche Nooden* (Fund for Foreign Needs) established in the seventeenth century to provide assistance to persecuted Mennonites in other parts of Europe.[12] Writing in the 1940s, Mennonite sociologist J. Winfield Fretz described MCC "as a glorious demonstration" of "mutual aid in a new day," a collaborative venture "that is much more complex than a barn raising or a husking but nevertheless a number of people working together to achieve a common goal," with the goal here being "to feed our brothers across the sea."[13]

Mutual aid within church communities, such as the barn raisings of Old Order Amish, depend on cultivated habits of sharing within the household of faith, while the mutual aid Fretz described at play in MCC's 1920s famine relief response expanded understandings of who belonged within the household of faith. Mutual aid within an expanding Mennonite household of faith in turn prepared Mennonites for sharing with a broader circle, with aid within the household of faith serving as training and preparation for, in Paul's words, doing good to all people.

The 1920s famine response did have a focus on Mennonite communities in southern Russia, but it also worked with those

---

[11] Ibid., 29-30.

[12] Unruh, *In the Name of Christ*, 356. For an account of the deeper and more recent history of Mennonite service preceding MCC's establishment, see Guy F. Hershberger, "Historical Background to the Formation of the Mennonite Central Committee," *Mennonite Quarterly Review* 44, no. 3 (July 1970): 213-244.

[13] Quoted in Marr, *The Transforming Power of a Century: Mennonite Central Committee and Its Evolution in Ontario* (Kitchener, ON: Pandora Press, 2003), 210.

Mennonite communities in extending relief assistance to non-Mennonites. To be sure, one factor behind this broader assistance was that Russian officials made such broader assistance a precondition for MCC's operations in the country. So, for example, MCC's agreements with Soviet officials do not speak of MCC providing assistance to Mennonites, but rather of MCC "rendering aid to the famine sufferers in Soviet Russia."[14] Similarly, an MCC letter to Herbert Hoover, the head of the American Relief Administration, the organization through which MCC aid was sent into Soviet Russia, presented MCC's relief program as a response to "the call of Russia for assistance," with MCC's program "receiving and forwarding funds and materials for war sufferers in South Russia."[15] "In keeping with pledges to the Russian government, aid was given without discrimination for race or creed," John Unruh observed in his 1952 history of MCC. Unruh proceeded to acknowledge, however, that "the efforts were designed to help especially the suffering 'brethren of the faith' and feeding operations were carried on in localities where Mennonites predominated."[16]

If, as the 1945 MCC silver anniversary booklet stated, "a major purpose of the M.C.C. relates to the desire of the American brotherhood to serve in behalf of fellow Mennonites both at home and abroad," it was also the case, the booklet continued, that "in a much larger way it [MCC] reaches out to all men everywhere, especially during times of national or world crises, such as wars."[17] P.C. Hiebert echoed this assessment in his foreword to the 1945 edition of the MCC Handbook, observing that since its foundation in July 1920, MCC had not only "found many opportunities to employ its good offices in the interest of our people," but had extended its field of activity "considerably

[14] "Agricultural Reconstruction Agreement—Appendix to Agreement between American Mennonite Relief and Russian Socialist Federative Soviet Republic," Oct. 1, 1921, in From the Files of MCC: The Mennonite Central Committee Story, Vol. 1, ed. Cornelius J. Dyck with Robert S. Kreider and John A. Lapp (Scottdale, PA: Herald Press, 1980), 25-26.

[15] Letter to Herbert Hoover, chairman, American Relief Administration, from Levi Mumaw, MCC Secretary-Treasurer, April 2, 1923, in From the Files of MCC, 27-28.

[16] Unruh, In the Name of Christ, 16.

[17] Twenty-Five Years, 3.

beyond the initial purpose of distributing food to those of the household of faith in famine-stricken Russia."[18] MCC had a dual responsibility, explained MCC board chair and Brethren in Christ leader C.N. Hostetter at the MCC annual meeting in 1944, a responsibility "both to those within and those without." "Within the world-wide fellowship of our Mennonite brotherhood, our duty seems clear to minister to the relief of human suffering," noted Hostetter. Yet, he stressed, "Our responsibility does not stop with those within the Mennonite brotherhood. As disciples of Christ, we must concern ourselves about human suffering wherever it is within the range of our possibility to help. True disciples of Christ must always remain sensitive and stand ready to minister and serve."[19] Or, in the Pauline language of Galatians, Mennonites might be called especially to do good to those within the household of faith, yet doing good should not stop at the boundaries of that household, but rather expand out to all people.

"That No Cause of Critical Need among Our People Goes Unmet"

In the years following the end of the Second World War, MCC embarked on what remains the largest response in its history, sending container after container of relief supplies for distribution among displaced persons and war-torn communities in post-war Europe. Within a year after the signing of the European armistice, MCC commissioned C.F. Klassen to investigate needs in Europe, with a focus on "the needs of the Mennonite brotherhood which was greatly affected by the war." Klassen highlighted the presence of displaced Mennonites from Russia in internment camps, which moved MCC "to bring aid to these stricken brethren."[20] The MCC response to the devastation of post-war Europe thus began with Mennonite co-religionists. In response to an October 1946 letter from 1st Lieutenant Roy Eluhow of the U.S. armed services asking MCC what could be done to assist displaced persons in post-war Germany from

---

[18] P.C. Hiebert, "Foreword," *MCC Handbook* (Akron, PA: MCC, 1945), 4, MCC U.S. archives, Akron, Pennsylvania.

[19] C.N. Hostetter, Jr., "Message from the Chairman," *MCC Workbook 1955* (Akron, PA: MCC, 1955), 1, MCC U.S. archives, Akron, Pennsylvania.

[20] *Twenty-Five Years*, 17.

Russia, Latvia, Poland, and Ukraine, MCC administrator William Snyder candidly responded that "Though we are interested in the plight of all unfortunate persons, we feel a particular responsibility to those of our number who belong to 'the same household of faith.'"[21]

However, while MCC in its post-war Europe response did undeniably have a special focus on responding to the needs of European Mennonite communities, MCC also sought, in the spirit of the Galatians passage, to do good to all people. An MCC administrator in 1945 observed that passions to proactively reach out beyond themselves to show Christian love in action through humanitarian relief had been kindled among Mennonites in the United States and Canada during the war years, writing that "The great and extensive need moved upon the hearts of the people, and . . . there is an increasing awareness of the excellent opportunity peace churches have to give a witness to Christian love through relief activities."[22]

Where possible, MCC sought to work in coordination with and through European Mennonite churches, even as the vast majority of MCC relief assistance was distributed through other channels. MCC relief worker Robert Kreider, based in Berlin, underscored in a July 1947 report on "Meeting Mennonite Need

Fig. 36: Robert Kreider, MCC representative, checks MCC relief supplies distributed through the Council of Relief Agencies Licensed for Operation in Germany (CRALOG) in 1947. Kreider was selected as one of CRALOG's representatives to oversee humanitarian aid distribution in the U.S.-controlled zone in Germany. (MCC photo)

---

[21] Letter from William Snyder to 1st Lieutenant Roy Eluhow, November 5, 1946, IX-06-03, Box 50, Folder 27/95, Mennonite Central Committee Correspondence 1945-1947 File 30 E Miscellaneous 1 1946, MCC U.S. archives, Akron, Pennsylvania.

[22] *Twenty-Five Years*, 18.

in Germany," that "Our concern is that no cause of critical need among our people goes unmet."[23] Citing the Galatians passage about doing good especially to those in the household of faith, Kreider explained that with "the help of organized committees of the Mennonites themselves, the MCC is seeking to help the needy among our brethren." Kreider conceded that providing this assistance to Mennonites in the different zones of occupied Germany "has not been any easy task": first, because Mennonites were "scattered" among the different zones; and second, because the "number of MCC workers who are authorized to do relief and refugee work among the refugees is very few," which meant that "the burden of work falls to the Mennonites themselves" in determining how to allocate relief aid. Kreider stressed that simply being Mennonite did not qualify a person for relief assistance: acute need was an essential criterion as well. "Our aim with the Mennonite [relief] committees is to seek out those Mennonites who have acute need and to aid them," Kreider explained. "Because a person has the label 'Mennonite' does not automatically entitle him to MCC relief aid. The Mennonite relief representatives work under the guiding principle that they must verify need before aid is given."[24] (fig. 36)

MCC also worked with the different European Mennonite relief committees not only to look inward to the needs of

---

[23] Robert Kreider, "Meeting Mennonite Need in Germany," July 1947, 3, IX-06-03, Box 59, Folder 32/60, Europe & Africa Project MCC Correspondence Kr 1947, MCC U.S. archives, Akron, Pennsylvania. Part of MCC's efforts to "meet Mennonite need" in post-war Europe involved seeking to prevent the return of displaced Mennonites to the Soviet Union and to help those Mennonites immigrate to South or North America. Multiple scholars over the past few decades have examined how, as part of these efforts, MCC workers downplayed the Germanic identity of the Mennonites who had fled the Soviet Union with retreating German forces while insisting that any Mennonite participation in the German military had been coerced, claims that recent scholarship disputes. See Ted Regehr, "Of Dutch or German Ancestry? Mennonite Refugees, MCC, and the International Refugee Organization," *Journal of Mennonite Studies* (1995): 7-25; Steven Schroeder, "Mennonite-Nazi Collaboration and Coming to Terms with the Past: European Mennonites and the MCC, 1945–1950," *Conrad Grebel Review* 21, no. 2 (2003): 6-16; and Benjamin Goossen, "From Aryanism to Anabaptism: Nazi Race Science and the Language of Mennonite Ethnicity," *Mennonite Quarterly Review* 90, no. 2 (2016): 135-163.

[24] Kreider, "Meeting Mennonite Need in Germany," 1.

Mennonite communities but also to reach out beyond themselves. Some European Mennonite relief committees moved in this direction—for instance, Kreider reported that a Mennonite relief committee in the French zone of occupied Germany led by Abram Braun and Emil Händiges had as its "first concern" ministering "to Mennonite need," but also noted that "their service extends to others in need who live in the vicinity of Mennonite congregations."[25] Yet Kreider also noted challenges in working with church groups that looked inward rather than outward. In a January 1947 letter to an MCC administrator in Akron, J.N. Byler, Kreider objected to what he termed "the limited relief spirit" of North American Baptists with whom MCC was partnering in relief efforts: "their exclusive concern with the needs of their 'particular household of faith'" represented a "narrow, sectarian relief philosophy" that "does not represent the full breadth of the spirit of Christian service," Kreider contended.[26] Kreider and his colleagues sought to counter what they sometimes viewed as a similarly sectarian relief approach among German Mennonites, insisting that "a program which is exclusively concerned with the household of faith does that household a disservice." "If we pumped all our supplies into the pantries of Mennonites they would love it," Kreider observed. "But the Mennonites would come out of the war despised by their neighbors, selfish and a pretty dim Christian witness. Our strategy to get the German Mennonites to organize themselves to help their needy cases and also to help others in need—is a more ennobling experience for them."[27]

[25] Ibid., 2.

[26] Robert Kreider to J.N. Byler, January 18, 1947, 1, IX-06-03, Box 59, Folder 32/66, Europe & Africa Project MCC Correspondence Kreider, Robert Dec - Feb 1947, MCC U.S. archives, Akron, Pennsylvania.

[27] Ibid., 2.

In Kreider's letter to Byler describing the dynamics at play between MCC and German Mennonites in making decisions about relief aid allocation, one sees a pattern that has repeated itself time and again over the past seventy years in MCC relief initiatives. MCC's church partners, both Anabaptist and non-Anabaptist, press for more relief aid to help those within those "household of faith" (even if the language from Galatians is not used). MCC in turn pushes back, to insist both on need as the fundamental criterion for who will receive relief assistance and on the importance of the church reaching out beyond itself. In such instances, MCC navigates the challenging rhetorical terrain of rightly insisting on upholding humanitarian principles in relief aid distribution while avoiding the danger of spiritual condescension potentially embedded in MCC, in Kreider's words, determining what will be a "more ennobling experience" for its church partners, a danger heightened by the power imbalance between a comparatively resource-rich MCC and its church partners.

Fig. 37: A young boy in Germany in 1947 or 1948 on his grandmother's lap holding a MCC-supplied can of meat. In 1947, forty-three workers were responsible for the distribution of 4,538 tons of food, clothing, and other supplies in Germany. In the summer of 1947, MCC was reaching approximately 80,000 people in feeding operations. (Original photo credit: Deutscher Zentralausschuss für die Verteilung ausländischer Liebesgaben beim Länderrat)

Even as it sought to counter what it sometimes viewed as a "sectarian" spirit among European Mennonites and other Christian groups, MCC also occasionally faced criticism from other Christian organizations of being overly focused on providing assistance to Mennonites (fig. 37). In May 1946, Ms. W.M. Berend, in her capacity as Secretary of the Inter-church Reconstruction Committee of the Netherlands, wrote to Peter Dyck, serving as MCC Director of Holland Relief, with complaints about MCC's failure to direct its relief aid

Fig. 38: Soup being served at a school in Germany, 1947-48, as part of MCC's post-WWII relief efforts. MCC participated in a joint child-feeding program that reached 72,000 children in eight cities in south-eastern Germany. (MCC photo/Heinz Wagener)

through the inter-church mechanism and about what Berend viewed as MCC's overly narrow focus on providing humanitarian assistance to Mennonites. Dyck responded defensively, asserting that "your accusation of our being sectarian in our distribution here and distributing only to our household of faith, the Mennonites, is entirely unfounded and unjust" and pointing to MCC's "Items of Accepted Policy" which stipulated "that the intent and influence of [MCC relief program] be to relieve need regardless of the recipient's race, class or political sympathies." (fig. 38) Granting that MCC had "direct contact with our Mennonite churches here and that often we distribute from Mennonite church buildings," Dyck emphasized that "statistics prove that much more is given to non-Mennonites than to Mennonites." Dyck arguably overstated his case when he insisted that "in our entire Relief program it is our intent and purpose to find out not the Mennonites but those people of all classes and all religions (and no religion) who are in greatest need": clearly MCC's post-war relief efforts in Europe did not use need as the sole criterion for assistance, but did also have a special concern for those of the Mennonite household of faith. Yet Dyck rightly noted that MCC cooperated with the Red

Cross and with municipal welfare authorities in the Netherlands in identifying aid recipients, with need serving as the basic criterion for those decisions (fig. 39).[28]

Fig. 39: Peter Dyck (left) helps to prepare a Christmas celebration for refugee children in Berlin, Germany, in 1947. (MCC photo)

"Our People's Vision Increased"

MCC's post-World War II response in Europe began a shift within MCC discourse away from a limited focus in relief efforts on fellow Mennonites. For Wilhelmina Kuyf of the MCC China Relief Unit, this meant developing a broader understanding of who belonged to the household of faith. Writing to MCC administrators William Snyder and J.N. Byler in 1947, Kuyf called for "Mennonite Aid" funds to be directed to meet emergency needs in China. Appealing to the Galatians passage, Kuyf argued for an expanded understanding of who qualified as belonging to the household of faith. Kuyf wrote: "As we think of the varied provision that has been made to help our [M]ennonite youth in the United States in their refusal to become part of the military machine, and other measures made to help refugee

---

[28] Letter from Peter J. Dyck, MCC Director of Holland Relief, to Miss W.M. Berend, Secretary of the Inter-church Reconstruction Committee of the Netherlands, June 7, 1946, IX-06-03, Box 50, Mennonite Central Committee Correspondence 1945-1947 File 30 Dyck Peter J. 1946, MCC U.S. archives, Akron, Pennsylvania.

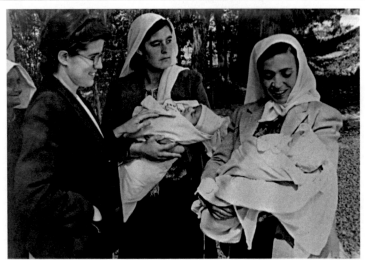

Fig. 40: MCC worker Geraldine Ebersole, left, and Palestinian refugee women in Jericho, West Bank, who received MCC newborn layettes in 1951. (MCC photo)

groups in our [M]ennonite fellowship, we realize that these Chinese are also our brothers and sisters in the household of faith."[29]

By the 1960s and 1970s, MCC leaders increasingly talked about an expanded vision of care and outreach on the part of Mennonites in the U.S. and Canada. MCC Executive Secretary William Snyder, in "Reflections on Christian Social Service" penned in 1963, admitted that "At times we were criticized for being too much concerned about our own people and not enough with the rest of the world," with MCC witness "restricted primarily to the brotherhood." While Snyder insisted that "there was always a concern for the welfare of the neighbor," he granted that this concern for doing good to all people had expanded over the past couple decades: "our people's vision increased as the modes of communication improved, as they grew more prosperous, and as they become more aware of human need on the national and international level. Now we are ministering to the needs of people of almost every race and creed and we are known around the world for

---

[29] Wilhelmina Kuyf to William Snyder and J.N. Byler, March 4, 1947, IX-06-03, Box 55, Folder 30/31, Europe & Africa Project MCC Correspondence Bl-Fq-China Office December-April 1947, MCC U.S. archives, Akron, Pennsylvania.

our ministry of compassion."[30] (fig. 40) Nine years later, in 1972, Canadian Brethren in Christ leader E.J. Swalm traced a similar trajectory of expanded vision. Although MCC workers of an earlier generation "were mindful of doing good to all [people]," observed Swalm, "they religiously specialized on 'the household of faith.'" Swalm continued that "In our generation, we are indebted to several factors that have not only aroused our brotherliness but have broadened our vision. They are the two global wars, modern communication, and speeds of travel." The "world has shrunk so much geographically," Swalm concluded, "that tragedy is close to us no matter where it occurs," in turn helping Mennonites in the U.S. and Canada come to a broader understanding of membership within the household of faith.[31] The Pauline qualification to do good especially to those within the household of faith now functioned in a less restrictive manner (fig. 41).

Fig. 41: Esther Thiessen, from Calgary, Alberta, standing to the extreme left, and Lydia Schlabach, from La Junta, Colorado, extreme right, hold babies at the Seoul Children's Relief Hospital in Korea in 1961. (MCC photo)

---

[30] William T. Snyder, "Reflections on Christian Social Service," MCC News Service, July 23, 1963, MCC U.S. archives, Akron, Pennsylvania.

[31] E.J. Swalm, "MCC (Canada)'s Conscience: Ventriloquism of the Soul," 2, presented at the 1972 MCC (Canada) Annual Meeting. January 14-15, 1972, MCC Canada Minutes #48. Mennonite Brethren Church, Steinbach, Manitoba, Feb. 4, 1972, MCC U.S. archives, Akron, Pennsylvania.

MCC vision and policy statements from the 1970s onwards embraced the humanitarian principle of impartiality. So, for example, the "MCC Statement on Program Assumptions, Objectives and Priorities" from 1976 highlighted that "our involvements throughout the world are rooted in our faithfulness to Christ who calls us to love and share with those in need regardless of race, creed or political persuasion."[32] The 1982 edition of the internal *MCC Handbook*, meanwhile, stressed that MCC "believes that help should be given without regard for religious or political persuasion." Granting that "MCC has felt a special sense of responsibility to aid fellow Christians—members of the household of faith—who may be stricken with calamity and suffering," the *Handbook* proceeded to insist that *need* is the "first" and "sole" criterion for aid: "MCC services everywhere are made available without regard to race, creed, nationality or social status of the recipients."[33] In a 1989 compilation of the "Unwritten Tenets of MCC Operations," MCC leader Reg Toews underscored that MCC was "responsive to the needs of everybody, not sectarian nor just for Mennonites."[34] In its 1994 statement, "A Commitment to Christ's Way of Peace," MCC declared that "Our love and ministry reach out to all, regardless of race, religion or status, whether friend or foe."[35]

The appeal to the Galatians passage, with its emphasis on especially doing good to the household of faith, markedly receded within MCC discourse from the 1960s onward, with the emphasis shifting more towards a clear embrace of the humanitarian principle of impartiality. Despite this shift, the tension between a call or an expectation to respond to needs

---

[32] "MCC Statement on Program Assumptions, Objectives and Priorities," January 24, 1976, A.6, in folder Docuware/Binational (BN) Minutes & Meeting Packets 1920 to 2012, Mennonite Central Committee Annual Meeting Minutes #382, January 22-24, 1976, 181-182, MCC U.S. archives, Akron, Pennsylvania.

[33] *MCC Handbook*, 17, 34, IX-40-04, Box 13, Folder 5, Folder title: MCC Handbooks 1950, 1954, 1972, 1980, 1982, 1987, MCC U.S. archives, Akron, Pennsylvania.

[34] Reg Toews, with Robert Kreider, "Unwritten Tenets of MCC Operations," #5, in folder Docuware/History & Research Requests/Toews, Reg Historical Study 1989, MCC U.S. archives, Akron, Pennsylvania.

[35] MCC, "A Commitment to Christ's Way of Peace," 1994, IX-40-04, Box 11, Folder 11/3, Folder title: Brochures 1994, MCC U.S. archives, Akron, Pennsylvania.

within the church, on the one hand, and the principle of basing humanitarian response on need alone, on the other, has nevertheless persisted.

An example from Nicaragua in the mid-1980s illustrates this enduring tension. In a memo entitled "What Should We Do?" MCC administrator Rich Sider asked for counsel about how to navigate MCC's relationships with the Nicaraguan Mennonite and Brethren in Christ churches. Sider observed that these churches held "an understanding of service that is primarily concerned with helping church members," something that created tension between the churches and MCC. In response to food needs within Nicaragua, MCC had decided to channel food aid through the Evangelical Committee for Aid and Development, or CEPAD, a Protestant ecumenical organization. "We wanted the food to be distributed through churches to the most needy displaced persons all over the country," Sider explained, and "CEPAD is the only organization with the capacity to do that, so we sent the food to them." While the Nicaraguan Mennonite and Brethren in Christ conferences belonged to CEPAD, they criticized MCC's decision to send aid through that channel. Sider reported: "the Mennonite churches say everyone in Nicaragua is suffering and that they have particularly needy people within their churches. But if they don't happen to be in areas where CEPAD is distributing, none of the food is available to them. They can't understand why we give so much to CEPAD and none directly to them. Besides, they say, CEPAD takes all the credit and doesn't mention that Mennonites have provided the resources so they don't even get any PR out of it. What should we do? How does the scriptural principle of 'first, the household of faith' apply here?" Sider asked. "What is more important, the family or the overall needs?"[36]

---

[36] Rich Sider, "What Should We Do? A Question from Central America," March 25, 1986, in 1986 Latin America Department, Nicaragua, Microfilm Reel 82, MCC U.S. archives, Akron, Pennsylvania.

Fig. 42: A relief distribution in 2014 by the Nigerian Church of the Brethren in Jos, Nigeria, to people displaced from northeastern Nigeria by the Islamist Boko Haram militia. (MCC photo/Dave Klassen)

Building Up and Expanding the Household of Faith

While the Galatians 6 passage has been rarely quoted within MCC over the past three decades, Sider's question about which takes precedence, the family or the overall needs, the particular or the universal, doing good to the household of faith or doing good to all, has persisted up until the present. In distributing humanitarian aid through the Syrian Orthodox church as it cares for people displaced by Syria's civil war, through the EYN (Church of the Brethren in Nigeria) as it ministers to communities facing attacks by the Islamist Boko Haram group (fig. 42), or via Conoglese Mennonite churches as they assist families uprooted by fighting in Congo's Kasai province, MCC continues to struggle with this tension between working with, through, and for the church and working solely based on the criterion of need. As discussed above, doing good especially to those within the church generates tensions—not necessarily irreconcilable tensions, but tensions nevertheless—with the humanitarian principle of impartiality. In the concluding part of this chapter, I shift focus to another dimension of MCC's work with the church, namely, how MCC has worked over the past century to build up and foster an expanded understanding of who belongs to the household of faith.

The very name, Mennonite Central Committee, already implies some type of ecumenical collaboration, a bounded set for which MCC operates as the center—or at least the center for the particular purpose of cooperative action by diverse Mennonite churches in feeding hungry people. To be sure, MCC has never operated as a Soviet-style central committee with top-down, centralized authority and the boundaries of the set of churches that claim MCC as their agency have been porous and shifting throughout MCC's history. MCC as an ecumenical, inter-Mennonite collaboration was at its inception a tentative one, a cooperative venture that has gained stability over time, but which has been and continues to be marked by different types of mutual suspicion and friction among Anabaptist churches. Henry Fast, an administrator of Civilian Public Service camps for MCC during World War II, captured one variation of these tensions as he reflected on the CPS program. "Our inter-Mennonite rivalries were, of course, a major problem in administering the CPS program," Fast wrote. "We were so jealous lest some group get an advantage. We had to make sure that we got proper representation in leadership as camp directors, business managers, cooks, and education directors. Who would visit the camps as ministers and to whom would they minister? And when ministers would offer communion, would it be to only the members of their own groups or would others be allowed to participate? We all had our stereotypes of one another. You mention somebody who is a Mennonite Brethren and you have one kind of image. And if you are from the General Conference, that stirs other feelings. They were a little bit afraid of G.C.s at that time because the stereotype said that G.C.s were worldly, activists, and liberal minded. We had to be very sensitive to the conservative groups."[37]

Yet even as divides of doctrine and practice have marked MCC from its beginnings, collaboration in service has fostered new forms of unity. Writing about MCC's relief distributions in Soviet Russia in the early 1920s, historian John Unruh reflected that beyond thousands being fed, clothed, and saved from starvation, there came from the initiative "a new sense of brotherhood on the part of those who administered the aid—a

---

[37] *Something Meaningful for God: The Stories of Some Who Served with MCC*, The Mennonite Central Committee Story, Vol. 4, ed. Cornelius J. Dyck, Robert S. Kreider, and John A. Lapp (Scottdale, PA: 1981), 55-56.

feeling of oneness in a common purpose that reached beyond the differences."[38] Similarly, he continued, the CPS alternative service program "brought the various Mennonite and affiliated groups into a co-operative relationship such as had never been attained before. True, the period of tremendous stress had its influence in this, but it was amazing how generally successful the whole program operated. The Mennonite Church in America more than ever before became aware of its strength."[39]

Such broadening of inter-Mennonite ecumenical horizons happened not only at the institutional but also the individual level. "When we were at home many of us lived largely to ourselves," reflected CPS participant Bennie Deckert in 1945. "We had very little contact with the outside world, with men of different denominations, occupations, different sects, communities and states. Our friends lived nearby, perhaps in our very local community. Now we know men from nearly every state, denomination, and from nearly all walks of life. To many of us Mennonites has come the realization that there is much more to the word Mennonite than is embodied in our own local group."[40]

Through the Civilian Public Service and Pax programs in the 1940s and 1950s, MCC actively sought to foster common theological convictions, particularly around the doctrine of nonresistance and the gospel of peace. The MCC Peace Section published multiple booklets on military conscription, aimed at shoring up Mennonite refusal of military service and at articulating a vision of nonresistance as an active witness to God's peace. MCC developed a curriculum for use in CPS camps of six booklets on Mennonite history, identity, and peace theology by Mennonite historians and theologians such as Harold S. Bender, C. Henry Smith, E.G. Kaufman, and Guy F. Hershberger, and organized regular peace conferences for Pax men in post-war Europe. Through such publishing and

---

[38] Unruh, *In the Name of Christ*, 22.

[39] Ibid., 267.

[40] Bennie Deckert, "Three Years in CPS," *Rising Tide* (June 1945): 3, IX-13-01, Box 15, Folder: MCC CPS Field Records Camp #33; Fort Collins, Colorado "The Rising Tide," Vol. 1 II-III, 1944-45, Folder Number 11/19, MCC U.S. archives, Akron, Pennsylvania.

Fig. 43: Members of Civilian Public Service Unit No.90 at Ypsilanti State Hospital in Ypsilanti, Michigan, in 1945 or 1946 discuss the church's involvement in hospitals for patients with mental illness. Participants included Lotus Troyer, Victor Janzen, and Gordon Kaufman (facing camera), along with Elmer Buhler, Lloyd Goering, Hubert Moore, and Karl Schultz. (MCC photo)

educational ventures, MCC not only brought people from theologically diverse Mennonite churches together in an ecumenism of practical collaboration in service, but also worked to nurture a shared identity and theological outlook. MCC's Peace Section sought over ensuing decades both to nurture peace theology and Anabaptist commitment to a gospel of peace, while also broadening peace theology conversations into ecumenical spheres (fig. 43).[41] MCC also at times pushed

---

[41] For several decades, MCC's Peace Section pioneered new directions in Anabaptist peace witness and peace theology rooted in MCC experiences. For accounts and analysis of the Peace Section, see John A. Lapp, "The Peace Mission of the Mennonite Central Committee," *Mennonite Quarterly Review* 44, no. 3 (July 1970): 281-297; Frank H. Epp and Marlene G. Epp. *The Progressions of Mennonite Central Committee Peace Section* (Akron, PA: Mennonite Central Committee, 1984); and "Seven Decades of MCC Peace Section," *Intersections: MCC Theory and Practice Quarterly* 1, no. 1 (Winter 2012): 7. Examples of publications from the Peace Section (and later Peace Office) that charted new directions in Anabaptist peace theology include John Richard Burkholder and Barbara Nelson Gingerich, eds., *Mennonite Peace Theology: A Panorama of Types* (Akron, PA: MCC Peace Office, 1991) and Duane K. Friesen and Gerald Schlabach, eds., *At Peace and Unafraid: Public Order, Security, and the Wisdom of the Cross* (Scottdale, PA: Herald Press, 2005).

Fig. 44: A choir composed of people living with HIV/AIDS who participated in an HIV/AIDS support group operated by the Meserete Kristos Church and assisted by MCC traveled from church to church in Ethiopia in 2006 to share the gospel through music and to reduce discrimination within the church against people living with HIV/AIDS. (MCC photo/Sarah Adams)

Mennonite churches on matters of theological ethics, challenging Mennonite churches through sponsored conferences, consultations, and publications to develop more robust peace theologies that went beyond the refusal of military service to also address racism, sexism, unjust economic systems, the criminal justice system, the human devastation of the natural environment, and the dispossession of Indigenous peoples, even as MCC also sometimes faced criticism from other Mennonites for being insufficiently bold in tackling justice issues.[42]

Representatives of the Peace Section and its successors contributed to and organized ecumenical consultations with the "historic peace churches" (Quakers, the Church of the Brethren, and Mennonites), the World Council of Churches, and others, from the so-called Puidoux conferences that ran between 1955 and 1962 that brought together mainline Protestants and members of the historic peace churches to discuss Christian peace theology to a series of global historic peace church consultations in the first decade of the twenty-first century parallel to the World Council of Churches' Decade to Overcome Violence.

[42] Examples of MCC newsletters and journals that broke new ground in practice-informed peace theology include: *Accord* (an MCC Canada newsletter about victim-offender ministries that ran from 1982 to 1998); *Conciliation Quarterly* (published by the MCC U.S. Mennonite Conciliation Service from 1982

MCC from its beginnings has also been a story of global Mennonite collaboration, not just collaboration among different Mennonite churches in the United States and Canada. MCC started in response to a call from Mennonites in southern Russia, with much of the staffing of the MCC-operated relief kitchens and feeding centers in the early 1920s coming from those communities. Following World War II, MCC partnered with European Mennonite churches in post-war relief and reconstruction. This partnership with Anabaptist churches has continued over subsequent decades to the present, from Zimbabwe to Congo to Ethiopia, from India to Nepal to South Korea, and from Bolivia to Colombia to Honduras (fig. 44).

Fig. 45: 2015 Teachers at Nakeempa Basic School in Choma district, Zambia, operated by the Zambian Brethren in Christ Church, take part in teacher training organized by MCC. (MCC photo/Michelle Potts)

In his 1952 history of MCC, John Unruh stressed that this inter-Mennonite "international co-operation has been encouraged, not

to 2005); *Liberty to the Captives* (a short-lived publication of the MCC Peace Section that examined alternatives to prison between 1972 to 1974); *Pathways* (an MCC Canada newsletter that highlighted "the healing journey of victims" of violent crime, issued between 1998 and 2002); the *Peace Office Newsletter* (a Peace Section and then Peace Office publication that appeared between 1971 and 2012); the *Washington Memo* (a publication of MCC's office in Washington, D.C., founded in the late 1960s and continuing today); and the *Women's Concerns Report* (initially a publication of the MCC Peace Section and then later MCC U.S. Peace and Justice Ministries, released between 1973 and 2004).

as an end in itself, but rather as mutually beneficial, and as an asset in certain efforts calling for concerted rather than individual action."[43] Yet one could argue that nurturing an expanded understanding of the Anabaptist-Mennonite faith has not simply been a byproduct of MCC's relief, development, and peacebuilding efforts, but has at times been an end in itself. MCC's leadership in building and maintaining connections with Mennonite communities behind the Iron Curtain during the Cold War, MCC's intertwined history with and extensive support for Mennonite World Conference, MCC's infrastructure of program offices around the world which provide an in-country point of contact for Mennonite churches in those countries with the broader Mennonite world even after North American mission agencies have scaled back or withdrawn their personnel—in these and other ways, MCC has worked to provide what MCC Executive Secretary William Snyder in 1963 called a "strong inter-Mennonite lift" to Anabaptist-Mennonite churches around the world (fig. 45).[44]

An integral part of MCC's mission "in the name of Christ" has thus been to nurture and expand common understandings of

Fig. 46: Salvadoran refugee children in the Mesa Grande refugee camp in Honduras in 1987. In October of that year, more than 4,000 refugees living in Honduras voluntarily returned to their home communities in El Salvador. MCC worked through Honduran churches to support these refugees. (MCC photo/Moses Mast)

43 Unruh, In the Name of Christ, 355.
44 Snyder, "Reflections on Christian Social Service," 4.

what it means to belong to the Anabaptist-Mennonite household of faith, be it through bringing different Anabaptist churches together in service to collaborate on practical relief, development, and peacebuilding projects, helping forge connections among various Mennonite churches, and advancing inter-Anabaptist peace theology as it responded to specific situations of violent conflict and injustice. A whole book, meanwhile, could be devoted to how over the decades MCC's broader-than-Anabaptist ecumenical partnerships have shaped, challenged, and expanded Mennonite understandings of who belongs to the household of faith—from collaboration with the Church of the Brethren and the Quakers in the establishment of Civilian Public Service during World War II, to support for ecumenical initiatives in Transkei in apartheid-era South Africa and in postcolonial contexts in East Africa, to partnerships with Coptic Orthodox and Coptic Evangelical churches in Egypt over the past forty years, to initiatives with Catholic communities and organizations working for justice within contexts of revolutionary change in Central America in the 1980s (fig. 46), to collaborations with Baptist and Pentecostal churches in humanitarian response in Ukraine today. Yet another book after that could address how MCC's relief, development, and peacebuilding engagements in interreligious contexts over the past sixty years have also raised questions for some MCCers about the scope and shape of the household of faith—from operating programs in countries like Bangladesh (fig. 47), Laos, and Vietnam with primarily non-Christian staff (from Muslim to Buddhist to Hindu and more), to collaboration with Islamic charitable societies in villages in rural Jordan, to the placement of students in universities behind the Iron Curtain during the Cold War and in Iran in the late 1990s and the early part of this century.[45] Through these ecumenical and interreligious engagements, MCC has encountered a wide variety of non-Christians heeding in their own distinctive ways Paul's call to do good to all people. These engagements have in turn raised

---

[45] For reflections on some of the interfaith engagements and collaborations carried out by MCC, see Alain Epp Weaver and Peter Dula, eds., *Borders and Bridges: Mennonite Witness in a Religiously Diverse World* (Telford, PA: Cascadia, 2007).

questions for MCC workers about how the Mennonite and broader Christian households of faith in turn relate to other households of faith. Such questions then point us back to the more basic question of what MCC's missiology is, what its understanding is of what it means to participate in God's reconciling mission in the world.

Fig. 47: MCC Bangladesh workers (from left) Russ Toevs, Derek D'Silva, Abdul Mannan, Kharibul Islam Khokon, Paul Shires, and Lee Brockmueller stand in a soybean field in western Bangladesh in 1982. (MCC photo/Russell Webster)

Chapter 5: Presence, Connection, Solidarity, Measurement: Missiologies in Tension in MCC

What does it mean to serve in the name of Christ? The previous chapters have explored different dimensions of that question through the case study of Mennonite Central Committee. Where does Christian service take place? What types of imagined landscapes does Christian service create? Who is understood to be engaged in Christian service? What regimes of power shape Christian service? How does a Christian service agency like MCC negotiate potential tensions between the humanitarian imperative to do good to all people and the more specific calling to support and work in, with, and through the church? These questions are *missiological* questions, questions that probe what it means to take part in God's mission to reconcile all of creation and humanity back to God. In this final chapter, I outline elements of a missiology for MCC today through an exploration of the conceptual frameworks MCC has used over the last five decades to describe its relief, development, and peacebuilding service. Or, more accurately, I examine what I argue are multiple missiologies in operation within MCC, missiologies that sometimes come into tension with one another.[1] I do so by focusing on specific keywords that reveal elements of MCC's missiology, keywords such as *presence*, *connect*, *solidarity*, and *measure*.

For some, talk of MCC's "missiology" might seem strange: words such as "mission" and "missiology" do not surface often within MCC's internal or external discourse. Writing in the early 1990s, MCC's international program director, Ray Brubacher, sought to fill what he viewed as a problematic gap by articulating a "missiology for MCC." Over the course of a year, Brubacher consulted widely within MCC, seeking to discern what explicit or implicit understandings of mission operated within MCC programs. MCC workers, Brubacher found, "seemed uncertain as to the nature of MCC's role as a church

---

[1] For a different exploration of multiple missiologies within MCC, see Stanley Green and James R. Krabill, "The Missiology of MCC: A Framework for Assessing Multiple Voices within the MCC Family," in *A Table of Sharing: Mennonite Central Committee and the Expanding Networks of Mennonite Identity*, ed. Alain Epp Weaver (Telford, PA: Cascadia, 2010), 192-212.

agency that does not plant churches," an uncertainty accompanied by defensiveness in the face of "criticisms of being 'skittish on mission' or 'anti-church.'"[2] MCC workers, Brubacher claimed, tended to associate "mission" and "missiology" with church-planting: with MCC not having a mandate to plant churches, it seemed to lack a missiology. Brubacher recognized that "not being expected to plant churches" was "in some ways, liberating" for MCC: "it allows us to have a reduced 'agenda,' to approach people more willing to listen and to work easily with a wide variety of local church partners and to move into areas where church planting is actually forbidden." That said, Brubacher continued, "just because we do not have a mandate to plant churches does not mean we should not have a missiology. We need a missiology as much as mission boards do. If we are confident in what our mission is," Brubacher argued, "we need not feel defensive or threatened when we discuss mission strategy" with other Mennonite agencies and "can give confident counsel" to Mennonite mission board colleagues "on how to go about kingdom work . . . and doing so without being dismissed, 'Well, that's just MCC . . . .'"[3] Brubacher recognized that even if MCC workers shied away from the words "mission" and "missiology," they still operated with unspoken and sometimes partially articulated understandings of what service in the name of Christ meant, and so were guided by implicit missiological assumptions. Making these assumptions explicit, Brubacher contended, would not only lead to more fruitful conversations with Mennonite mission agencies but also lend greater coherence and confidence to MCC service.

Brubacher's project in the early nineties of seeking to lay the groundwork for a future MCC missiology reflected a broader desire within MCC to make foundational assumptions more explicit. So, for example, in 1989, MCC leader Reg Toews, with assistance from Robert Kreider, compiled a set of what he called the "unwritten tenets of MCC's operations," an attempt to foreground implicit dimensions of MCC's program. Several of these 29 tenets captured MCC's implicit missiology. An implicit

---

[2] Ray Brubacher, "A Missiology for MCC," *Intercom* 35, no. 9 (October 1991): 8.
[3] Ibid.

Fig. 48: In this 1979 photo in Feni, Bangladesh, MCC workers Ali Mia (left) and George Klassen experiment with a mechanical suction chamber attached to a cast-iron pump, one of many experiments that eventually led to the creation of the rower pump technology. (MCC photo/Charmayne Brubaker)

missiology was perhaps appropriate for an organization "inclined," in Toews' words, "toward a quiet witness in the name of Christ." MCC programs, Toews explained, were "personnel intensive," with people, rather than money or material aid, being "MCC's most important contribution." (fig. 48). The people MCC sent, meanwhile, did not arrive in communities with pre-determined plans or strategies: instead, Toews stressed, MCC operated more as "the facilitator of ideas and concerns than the generator of ideas and concerns," a stance that paired well with what Toews described as an "inclination to second workers to other agencies," with the strategy of worker secondment "reflecting a commitment to working through indigenous structures and [a] commitment to servanthood."[4]

Supportive partnerships, mutual relationships, the quiet witness of presence: these unwritten tenets of MCC's operations identified by Toews in 1989 had become increasingly explicit by the summer of 1992, when my spouse, Sonia, and I prepared to leave the United States to teach English at a Catholic school in the village of Zababdeh in the north of the occupied West Bank:

[4] Reg Toews, with Robert Kreider, "Unwritten Tenets of MCC Operations," #7, 3, 18, and 23, in folder Docuware/History & Research Requests/Toews, Reg Historical Study 1989, MCC U.S. archives, Akron, Pennsylvania.

in communications with our supervisors and at orientation in Akron, Pennsylvania, we repeatedly heard a consistent message from MCC about the nature of our assignment, namely, that MCC was sending us to be *present* in the village—to immerse ourselves in the daily patterns of village life, to gain Arabic language skills, and to learn and appreciate Palestinian culture. We were not sent with a predetermined agenda but were instead tasked with building connections and forging relationships, accompanying one Palestinian community living under and resisting a military occupation regime that received major financial support from our own U.S. government. Presence, solidarity, connection, relationship, accompaniment: these were the keywords of the MCC missiology that shaped our orientation to MCC. Our pre-assignment orientation in Akron, Pennsylvania, focused on building cultural adaptation skills and stressed the importance of approaching new contexts with open ears, an inquisitive spirit, and a readiness to learn.

What our orientation did not focus on, however, was equipping us with pedagogical techniques and strategies to carry out our assignment as English teachers, nor on the importance of helping students achieve educational goals. Yet, as we quickly discovered, the administrators, teachers, parents, and students at the school to which we had been assigned viewed our primary purpose not as being a listening presence within the village, but as teaching, and they expected concrete results from that teaching, in the form of greater student fluency in reading, writing, and speaking English, including as measured by government exams. The mission focus on accompaniment, presence, and solidarity thus came quickly into tension with the need in our individual assignment to plan for, continuously monitor, and evaluate our success in teaching our students English. The tension we faced in our first MCC assignment in holding together the missiological imperative of being present, on the one hand, with the need to plan for and report on results, on the other, is a tension that has defined MCC more broadly over the past two or three decades. In the concluding section of this chapter, I reflect on how the drive to plan for and measure results in MCC's work sits with MCC missiologies of presence, a question that in turn brings us back to the place of power in Christian service: who exercises it, where is it located, and how does power shape understandings of what it means to serve?

Accompaniment, Presence, and Relational Programming

But before turning to those questions, I first trace the emergence within MCC program in the seventies and eighties of an emphasis on presence and accompaniment. In chapter 3, I examined how, starting in the 1970s, MCC began to reconceptualize service in terms of listening to and waiting with the communities in which MCCers worked. This shift in how to understand service went hand-in-hand with another shift, a shift from MCC directly implementing projects to supporting projects planned and implemented by local churches and community-based organizations. The seeds of this shift were planted in the 1960s, as MCC leaders rethought mission patterns in light of post-colonial realities. "Some overseas efforts in missions and relief have been characterized by a paternalism similar to the attitude of western nations in the so-called colonial period," observed MCC Executive Director William Snyder in 1963. "The winds of change toward political independence have likewise affected the churches and mission programs in the underdeveloped countries. Missionaries and relief workers today must adopt a true servant relationship to these younger churches . . ." Snyder concluded.[5] Painting with very broad strokes, MCC program director Edgar Stoesz wrote in 1976 in MCC's internal publication *Intercom* that "North American agencies used to go around running their own programs, using their own personnel and doing pretty well as they pleased. Eventually the error of that approach became obvious and we began to have a great deal of respect for the indigenous process. Now," Stoesz concluded, "we much prefer to identify an existing agency with which we feel compatible and support it with personnel or money, permitting it to enlarge its effort."[6] Also in 1976, MCC's board affirmed the importance of learning from

---

[5] William T. Snyder, "Reflections on Christian Social Service," 3, MCC News Service, July 23, 1963, MCC U.S. archives, Akron, Pennsylvania.

[6] Edgar Stoesz, "An Improvement, Yet a Dilemma," *Intercom* 16, no. 7 (July 1976): 1-2.

and supporting local organizations. "Our involvements will take place in a spirit of mutual respect, realizing that we must put as much effort into learning as we do into teaching," the board declared.[7] Instead of viewing development as a unilateral process in which knowledge and skills are transferred from agencies like MCC to communities in so-called underdeveloped countries, this MCC board statement instead presented development as "based on local capacity and self-reliance."[8]

From the late seventies into the nineties, these emerging understandings of development within MCC steadily gained traction. MCC leaders increasingly began describing this listening stance of service with the language of "presence" or the slightly more active vocabulary of "partnership" and "accompaniment." Several interconnected and mutually reinforcing factors contributed to this shift. First, MCC experiences in the 1960s in post-colonial contexts in which nationalist movements in newly independent countries charted new visions for national liberation and development pushed MCC to begin revisioning how it positioned itself in these contexts, stepping back from viewing itself as a lead agent for change to instead recognize that the primary energies and leadership for change came from within communities themselves. Second, the rise in the seventies and eighties of civil society organizations such as farmers' associations, women's cooperatives, and social service agencies of national churches in many parts of the global South pressed MCC to consider how it could support and accompany these organizations as they worked to make change in their communities. Many MCC programs began to shift in this period away from directly implementing program towards partnership with local churches, church agencies, and community-based organizations. Third, within broader missiological circles, a rethinking of Christian mission was gaining steam, with a shift in emphasis away from sending missionaries from the global North to the global South

---

[7] "MCC Statement on Program Assumptions, Objectives and Priorities," January 24, 1976. A.3, in folder Docuware/Binational (BN) Minutes & Meeting Packets 1920 to 2012, Mennonite Central Committee Annual Meeting Minutes #382, January 22-24, 1976. 18, 181-182, MCC U.S. archives, Akron, Pennsylvania.

[8] Ibid., B.3.

toward a focus on how churches in both the global North and the global South might together join in the *missio Dei*, God's reconciling mission in the world. This transformation of mission thinking meant a disruption of paternalistic relationships between European and North American mission agencies, on the one hand, and churches in the global South, on the other, and the beginning of halting efforts to develop mutual mission partnerships between the churches of the global North and the global South.[9] Finally, the failure of modernization theory to live up to its promises led MCC and other international development actors in the seventies and eighties to reassess their development models and search for alternatives. While modernization theory had held that countries of the global South would accrue steadily expanding benefits and improved livelihoods through the adoption of Western-style institutions in the realms of education, health, and economic systems, reality did not live up to the heralded vision.[10]

Development initiatives informed by modernization theory depended on centralized interventions by the state or external agencies, such as the United Nations or international non-governmental organizations like MCC. As a counter to such top-down development, MCC program leaders began in the 1970s championing visions of development as emerging from community-led and community-owned processes. In a series of "Development Monographs" and in several Occasional Papers released in the seventies and eighties, MCC leaders like Edgar Stoesz, Nancy Heisey, and Tim Lind advanced this bottom-up mode of development while critiquing the optimism that drove modernization theory. So, for example, in surveying the

---

[9] See, for example, David Bosch, *Transforming Mission: Paradigm Shifts in Theology of Mission* (Maryknoll, NY: Orbis Books, 1991).

[10] For discussions and analysis of MCC's community development efforts within the broader context of shifting development discourses, see Robb Davis, "MCC's Development Paradigm(s)," in *A Table of Sharing: Mennonite Central Committee and the Expanding Networks of Mennonite Identity*, ed. Alain Epp Weaver (Telford, PA: Cascadia, 2010), 339-352 and Bruce Guenther and William Reimer, in "Relationship, Rights, and 'Relief': Ninety Years of MCC's Integrated Response to Humanitarian Crises," *A Table of Sharing: Mennonite Central Committee and the Expanding Networks of Mennonite Identity*, ed. Alain Epp Weaver (Telford, PA: Cascadia, 2010), 353-374.

development programs promoted across Africa from the 1950s into the 1970s, MCC Africa director Lind highlighted the "continuing failure of planning to accurately predict consequences of specific actions or to foresee new problems created by new technology." These ongoing failures, Lind underscored, should "temper" any residual optimism about the efficacy of such centralized development measures.[11]

Not only did development efforts based on modernization theory fail to live up to their promises, argued Lind, they were actively harmful, corroding traditional community ties and mechanisms of social support, effectively sorting "out the weak at one extreme and the strong at the other." Development-as-modernization was atomizing, Lind continued, releasing "individuals from traditional community restraints" by pushing "the able to excel." By having as its ultimate goal "integration into 'the world' through modernization," Lind concluded, "development works against community."[12]

Countering models that equated development with industrialization, modernization, and Westernization, MCC program leaders in the seventies and eighties drew upon the work of the Brazilian educator, Paulo Freire, and his notion of *conscientization*, a pedagogy of popular consciousness-raising in which students, not teachers, are viewed as the primary actors in the learning process.[13] Reflecting on what she described as the failure of school systems set up by missionary and colonial authorities in Africa to deliver Western-style development, MCC Africa program leader Nancy Heisey turned to Freire's idea of conscientization as well as to the notion of deschooling advanced by the Austrian-Croatian priest and educator, Ivan Illich, to promote an understanding of education and development as community-led processes, rather than primarily as interventions organized by the state or by international actors (fig. 49).[14]

---

[11] Tim Lind, *Biblical Obedience and Development*, Development Monograph Series No. 6 (Akron, PA: MCC, 1977-78), 19.

[12] Ibid., 20.

[13] Paulo Freire, *Pedagogy of the Oppressed*, trans. Myra Ramos (New York: Continuum, 1970).

[14] Nancy Heisey, *Integrating Education and Development*, Development

Fig. 49: MCC workers Todd Benson (background) and Nancy Heisey (center) join a farmer in Chad in 1985 to check the level of diguettes (dikes), which slowed rainwater run-off from planted fields which allowed moisture to soak into the earth. (MCC photo/David and Justine Foxall)

Edgar Stoesz also built on Freire's work in defining development as "a people's struggle in which the poor and oppressed are the active participants and beneficiaries," a "conscientization process by which people are awakened to opportunities within their reach." Instead of requiring external intervention, development emerging from conscientization, Stoesz argued, "begins as an attitude in the hearts and minds of people," building on their existing knowledge and driven by their own initiative.[15]

Merrill Ewert, who served as project coordinator for MCC in the mid-seventies in what was then Zaire, also drew from Freire's pedagogy of critical consciousness-raising in order to articulate a model of development education that did not "contribute to domination." Such a Freirian model of development, Ewert explained, reconceptualized the role of MCC workers to be "facilitators instead of manipulators,"

Monograph Series No. 5 (Akron, PA: MCC, 1977). See Ivan Illich, *Deschooling Society* (New York: Harper and Row, 1971).

[15] Edgar Stoesz, *Thoughts on Development*, Development Monograph Series No. 1 (Akron, PA: MCC, revised edition, 1977), 3-4.

people who did "not control decisions or the flow of information," but rather helped "create optimal conditions in which the local people can determine their own direction." In this development model, Ewert continued, "there are no teachers and learners, advisors and advisees, or experts and laypeople— all work together to solve problems."[16]

For MCC, adopting a model of development as conscientization meant reconfiguring its own place in the development process, taking a step back from seeing itself as leading or controlling the development process and instead viewing itself as supporting and accompanying locally-led efforts. "Outside agencies do not bring development," Stoesz emphasized. Rather, he continued, development "is an indigenous process going on before [agencies like MCC] arrive. At best they accelerate its pace; at worst they frustrate it."[17] Agencies like MCC, Tim Lind cautioned, "must from the very beginning abdicate the executive power inherent in its position as implementor or planner."[18] Rather than building up their own profile or controlling development processes, Stoesz argued, the "highest goal" for MCC and other international development organizations should be "to strengthen institutions which are locally owned."[19]

MCC programs in Africa took the lead in adopting accompaniment and partnership models of development. Beginning in Lesotho in 1980, MCC programs in Africa started shifting away from direct implementation of relief and development initiatives towards what MCC Africa director Tim Lind called "relational programming," or a "community worker movement." Spurred by what Lind and others within MCC viewed as the "failure of development activity" and by a "disillusionment with development institutions," MCC programming in Africa transitioned towards a model of "presence," involving the long-term placement of MCC workers within local communities, outside of institutional contexts, and

[16] Merrill Ewert, *Humanization and Development*, Development Monograph Series No. 2 (Akron, PA: MCC, 1975), 25.

[17] Edgar Stoesz, *Thoughts on Development*, 12.

[18] Tim Lind, *Biblical Obedience and Development*, 28.

[19] Edgar Stoesz, *Thoughts on Development*, 11.

"with an emphasis on learning about and developing relationships with specific communities and their needs." These "community worker" placements, Lind stressed, were not primarily focused on technical implementation of projects, but were rather shaped by a "learning stance *vis-à-vis* Africans." This missiology of presence started from the assumption that "program creativity and renewal" came not from MCC but rather from African communities themselves. MCC's organizational stance within this vision of relational programming was a servanthood posture towards African churches. Adopting such a posture, Lind stressed, was a "better way for us to participate in and respond to problems faced by Africans."[20]

If this shift away from implementation toward presence and partnership began within MCC's programs in Africa, it quickly expanded to other parts of the MCC world. So, for example, the 1980s witnessed the establishment of an MCC rural development program in the Artibonite Valley in Haiti. This program wedded a Freirean pedagogy of conscientization with the Haitian tradition of communal work days (*konbits*). Members of MCC's Haitian animation team took on facilitating rather than teaching roles as they engaged isolated rural communities in Haiti's rolling mountains and valleys in agricultural development initiatives. In a 1989 paper describing the MCC Haiti team's approach, Barry Bartel explained that animation entailed a facilitative process in which community members themselves identified their gifts, resources, and needs and took the lead in developing and implementing responses to those needs, with MCC playing a supportive role. "With their own planning, work, and sacrifice," Bartel contended, "[Haitian communities] will own the solution, begin to feel like they can solve their own problems, and work to ensure that the solution lasts," with positive impacts continuing long after MCC animators had left the community.[21]

---

[20] Tim Lind, *MCC Africa Program: Historical Background*, MCC Occasional Paper No. 10 (Akron, PA: MCC, August 1989), 19.

[21] Barry C. Bartel, *Animation in Haiti: MCC Haiti's Experience with Rural Community Development*, MCC Occasional Paper No. 8 (Akron, PA: MCC, 1989), 1-2.

By the end of the 1980s, this missiology of presence and partnership had taken root in MCC orientations of new workers and in most MCC programs. In his report to the governing board in 1987, MCC executive secretary John A. Lapp explained that "A ministry of presence suggests that need is best defined from the stance of being present rather than by strategies inspired by well-developed ideology, media headlines or grandiose projects."[22] While in modernization models of development the state and international aid organizations led the design and implementation of large-scale initiatives to improve education, health, and livelihoods, in the accompaniment and presence models of development, MCC took a step back, seeking to support and follow the lead of local churches and community-based organizations. A desire not to overwhelm and usurp local leadership, Reg Toews observed, in turn led to a "preference for the small scale. If you make mistakes, let them be little mistakes."[23]

Connecting, Dismantling, and Mutual Transformation

A missiology of presence was essential, people like Stoesz, Heisey, Ewert, and Lind argued, for relief, development, and peacebuilding efforts to be sustainable. The connections forged through service as presence, however, also came to be viewed as ends in themselves. The stress on presence and people within MCC programs reflected what Reg Toews in 1989 described as a growing "commitment to reciprocity, exchange, partnership— seeking the grace of being able to receive gifts as well as give gifts."[24] Service was not viewed as a unilateral movement from the strong to the weak. Instead, service came to be viewed as an exercise in "connecting peoples," building connections across lines of national, cultural, religious, racial, and class difference (fig. 50).

---

[22] John A. Lapp, "Report of the Executive Secretary," *MCC Workbook Report*, 1987, 2, in folder Docuware/Workbook 1944 to 2011/1987 Workbook, MCC U.S. archives, Akron, Pennsylvania.

[23] Reg Toews, with Robert Kreider, "Unwritten Tenets of MCC Operations," #15.

[24] Ibid., #14.

While the specific phrase "connecting peoples" does not surface within MCC's internal discourse until the late nineties and the early aughts, the idea had deep roots within MCC's history. As discussed in the previous chapter, building ecumenical connections across the Anabaptist-Mennonite world has arguably been a core element of MCC's work since its inception, rather than peripheral to or a byproduct of its efforts. Similarly, then, MCC came to view the relationship-building by MCC workers as they sought to accompany and be present in marginalized communities around the world not simply as an effective development approach, but also as an end in itself. Such relationship-building opened up the possibility for what MCC called *mutual transformation*. Mutual, mutuality, mutually-

Fig. 50: In 1993, MCC worker Jeanne Zimmerly Jantz harvests squash seeds with women members of a farmer's group in Zaire (now Democratic Republic of the Congo). (MCC photo/Dan Jantzi)

transformative relationships: such vocabulary was ubiquitous within MCC during the nineties and the aughts. So, for example, MCC's 1999 statement on the *Principles that Guide Our Mission* highlighted that "MCC serves as a channel of interchange by building relationships that are mutually transformative" and that "MCC facilitates interchange and mutual learning between

MCC Logos Throughout the Years

1941 - 1943   1943 - ca. 1960?

ca. 1960 - 1970?   1970 – Present

Fig. 51. The evolution of MCC's logo. Courtesy of MCC U.S. archives, Akron, Pennsylvania.

its supporting constituency and those with whom we work around the world, so that all may give and receive."[25]

A look at the evolution of MCC's logo offers a window onto the changing role of relationships within MCC discourse (fig. 51). In MCC's first logo, which was used for just two years in the early 1940s, and then also in its second logo, used from the early forties through the fifties, one sees clasped hands in front of the cross, but with the clasped hands at an angle, one hand reaching up in need and the other hand reaching down to offer assistance.

---

[25] *Principles that Guide Our Mission* (Akron, PA: MCC, 1999).

The clasped hands embody a relationship, but an asymmetrical one, a relationship marked by the power to give. In 1960, however, MCC adopted a new logo, still with clasped hands in front of the cross, but now with the hands positioned level, shaking in partnership. One can see in this third MCC logo an emerging understanding of service not as the unilateral action of those reaching down to help those in need, but as founded on relationships of mutuality and common need before the cross.

While the clasped hands disappear from the current MCC logo, adopted in 1970, the idea of mutual relationship-building as central to MCC's identity, as embodied by the clasped hands before the cross, only deepened over the ensuing decades.[26] A missiology of presence not only opened space for local visions and initiatives to flourish: it opened space for MCC workers to recognize their own need, a space for a transformed understanding of themselves not as self-sufficient persons who give from a position of strength, but as persons also marked by need of different kinds, persons who need the gifts that others can share with them. In this missiological model, MCC service thus becomes entry into a space of mutual sharing and transformation.

In its 1994 statement outlining "A Commitment to Christ's Way of Peace," MCC articulated this understanding of service as mutual gift-sharing thus: "We recognize our own spiritual and moral poverty and seek to receive the gifts that others, some of whom may be materially poorer than we are, have to share with us."[27] The next couple of decades expanded this conception of service as mutual relationship-building beyond relationship-building between people from Canada and the U.S., on the one hand, and communities in the global South, on the other. Even with the emphasis on mutuality, the danger loomed that people from the U.S. and Canada would still be foregrounded, just now

---

[26] For discussions of MCC's logo and visual identity, see Jonathan Dyck, "MCC and Visual Identity," *Intersections: MCC Theory and Practice Quarterly* 6, no. 4 (Fall 2018): 3-5 and Robert S. Kreider and Rachel Waltner Goossen, "Reporting the MCC Experience: Images and Posters," in *Hungry, Thirsty, a Stranger: The MCC Experience* (Scottdale: Herald Press, 1988), 193-209.

[27] "A Commitment to Christ's Way of Peace," #3, 1994, IX-40-04, Box 11, Folder 11/3, Folder title: Brochures 1994, MCC U.S. archives, Akron, Pennsylvania.

in their need for transformation. The expansion of the International Volunteer Exchange Program (IVEP), founded in 1953, from a program that initially focused on exchange opportunities for European Mennonite young adults in the U.S. and Canada into a service program in Canada and the U.S. for young adults primarily from the global South, revealed that relationship-building did not only have to flow *from* the U.S. and Canada *to* the global South. The multi-directional flow of connections and relationship-building through service became truly globalized, however, with the establishment in 2004 of the Young Anabaptist Mennonite Exchange Network (YAMEN), in partnership with Mennonite World Conference, in which young adults from the global South go to serve in other parts of the global South, with connections and relationships built across the global Anabaptist church through such service (fig. 52).

Fig. 52: Damaris Guaza Sandoval, a 2017-2018 Young Anabaptist Mennonite Exchange Network (YAMEN) participant from Colombia, facilitates a workshop on self-esteem for a fourth-grade class at the Francisco Morazán school in La Ceiba, Honduras. (MCC photo/Ilona Paganoni)

Globalized modes of relatively fast and inexpensive transportation and communication have increased opportunities for global connection, especially for persons from the wealthier countries of the global North. Seeking to respond to global needs, Christians from Canada and the U.S., Mennonites included, have sought opportunities to help through various types of short-term missions trips, especially in Central America and the Caribbean, given their proximity to the U.S. and Canada. Yet the extensive critiques of such short-term missions have highlighted how they threaten to devolve into harmful poverty tourism that reinforces paternalistic and hierarchical relationships in which self-sufficient persons from the global North deign to reach down to help persons in the global South. In the eighties and nineties, MCC staff in Central America like Elaine Zook Barge and Daryl Yoder-Bontrager gave sustained

Fig. 53: Ernie Engbrecht (left), Annie Engbrecht, and other members of an MCC Alberta learning tour to Nepal inaugurate a drinking water tap in Khijifalate village, Okhaldhunga district, built by MCC partner, SAHAS (Group of Helping Hands), and its community-based member organization, Likhu Demba Community Development Forum (LDCDF). (MCC photo/Avash Karki)

attention to how the desire and passion for such mission trips on the part of Mennonites in Canada and the U.S. might be channeled into opportunities not for unidirectional service but instead for connection and learning. Building on their experiences in organizing what they called "learning tours" and "work and learn teams," Zook Barge, Yoder-Bontrager, and others compiled a *Connecting Peoples* manual in 2003 that provided guidance on how to organize short-term learning opportunities that carried with them the possibilities of transformation, "opportunities," in Zook Barge's words, "that help us *look* at new issues and places, *listen* to different voices, *learn* from each other and *live* in ways that create a more just, humane, sustainable and peaceful world."[28] (fig. 53).

One type of connection forged within MCC service by being present has been the connection of solidarity. A 1976 MCC board statement underscored the expectation of MCC workers "being in solidarity and identifying with the weak and oppressed."[29] A 1982 consultation organized by MCC Ontario on Native Ministries, meanwhile, reported that Indigenous First Nations leaders in Canada had counseled MCC not "to be just another

Fig. 54: Paul Quiring observes a 1978 distribution of olive tree seedlings to Palestinian farmers in the West Bank. MCC distributed thousands of the seedlings to farm families in the Ramallah, Bethlehem, and Hebron districts of the West Bank as part of its rural development program inaugurated in 1976. (MCC photo)

social service agency," but rather to "become partners in the cause," with Indigenous leaders stressing that "'being there' as companions was a political act."[30]

---

[28] Elaine Zook Barge, "Connecting People: MCC, Exchange and the Possibility of Transformation," *Intersections: MCC Theory and Practice Quarterly* 8, no. 4 (Fall 2020): 23-25.

[29] "MCC Statement on Program Assumptions, Objectives and Priorities," B.4.

[30] MCC Ontario consultation on Native Ministries, November 1982, quoted in

Connection-as-solidarity was, to be sure, fraught with challenges and complications. What, MCCers wondered, did solidarity look like in contexts of stark oppression and revolutionary change like apartheid-era South Africa, the occupied Palestinian territories, and Central America in the 1980s (fig. 54)? In 1985 "Guidelines for Mennonite Central Committee Workers in Contested Areas," William Snyder, Earl Martin, and Atlee Beechy counseled "maintaining connections with all segments of the population in the contested area to the degree possible and quietly interpreting MCC purposes."[31] Yet MCCers sometimes found that partisanship amidst conflict was hard to avoid. So, for example, Susan Classen reflected in the mid-eighties from a village in El Salvador that "The people I work with have clearly chosen the side of the revolution. As a matter of fact, it would be more accurate to say that they are the revolution."[32] Gerald Schlabach, working with MCC in Nicaragua, observed that "the church has taught, and the sending agency has encouraged, the field worker to 'identify with the poor and the suffering.' Now, however, the poor are to some extent identifying with an armed revolutionary struggle and organization. What next?" asked Schlabach.[33] In apartheid-era South Africa, meanwhile, MCC workers Robert Herr and Judy Zimmerman Herr asked "Who interprets South Africa?" for MCC, when the church in South Africa contained "both oppressors and oppressed, those who bless the status quo and those who suffer under or work to change it."[34] A commitment to accompanying the church and marginalized peoples now led

---

Lucille Marr, *The Transforming Power of a Century: Mennonite Central Committee and Its Evolution in Ontario* (Kitchener, ON: Pandora Press, 2003), 254.

[31] "Guidelines for Mennonite Central Committee Workers in Contested Areas," William Snyder, Earl Martin, Atlee Beechy, June 1985, 6, in Overseas Headquarters Manual, 1988, microfilm 1988 Roll #130 Folder title: Overseas Headquarters Manual folder, MCC U.S. archives, Akron, Pennsylvania.

[32] Susan Classen, "A Response from El Salvador," in Gerald Schlabach, *Identification with the People in a Revolutionary Situation*, MCC Occasional Paper No. 2 (Akron, PA: MCC, May 1988), 16.

[33] Gerald Schlabach, *Identification with the People in a Revolutionary Situation*, MCC Occasional Paper No. 2 (Akron, PA: MCC, May 1988), 1.

[34] Robert Herr and Judy Zimmerman Herr, *Listening to the Church: Mennonite Ministry in South Africa*, MCC Occasional Paper No. 3 (Akron, PA: MCC, June 1988), 43.

MCC workers to grapple with how to live as a nonviolent witness to God's love while also standing in solidarity with people revolting against and resisting violent and oppressive regimes.

Attempts to be fully present among and identify and stand in solidarity with poor, marginalized, and oppressed communities also challenged MCC workers to consider the privilege they carried, privilege they could not simply wish away. After serving several years with MCC in Appalachia in the mid-1980s, Carol Loeppky wondered if total presence in and identification with marginalized communities were unattainable goals. "I

Fig. 55: Homeowner Junellen (center) shares a laugh with Rick Gallimore (left) and Lee McGlaghlin, participants in MCC's Serving with Appalachian People (SWAP) program. Gallimore and McGlaghlin, part of a group from Gettysburg Foursquare Church in Gettysburg, Pennsylvania, helped repair the roof of Junellen's house in Dema, Kentucky. (MCC photo)

suppose many people enter voluntary service with some notion of forsaking worldly possessions and perspectives to identify with the poor. I also had some of those ideals. Now I think that ideal is unrealistic," Loeppky confessed. "I believe that no matter what my intentions, the gap between me and the poor will never close or even narrow perceptibly." Loeppky reflected that her education and family support system provided her with financial and other resources that always left a gap between her and the people in the low-income Appalachian communities where she lived and worked with MCC. These structural realities, she concluded, meant that "my attempt at identification with the poor is a weak attempt."[35] (fig. 55)

Forging mutual connections across divisions of nationality, class, race, and religion in turn spurred MCC workers from Canada and the U.S. to push for change within their home countries, to dismantle and transform lifestyles and structures that perpetuated injustice at home and abroad. In 1976, MCC's board declared that part of MCC's mission was "To sensitize our constituency to the injustices and human suffering which exist at home and abroad, so that the church can participate in MCC ministries with greater understanding and follow a life style commitment consistent with Biblical and Anabaptist principles."[36] MCC's global work in the seventies among communities facing famine and hunger globally led MCC to engage its Anabaptist supporters in Canada and the U.S. about how their own lifestyles participated in a destructive global economy and about the imperative of conforming individual and communal lives to gospel imperatives of joy within simplicity, an engagement exemplified by the *More-with-Less* cookbook and the companion guide with ideas for *Living More-with-Less*. Gord and Tillie Hunsberger, MCC workers in Grande Rivière du Nord, Haiti, explained in 1977 that "We experience frustrations when we see such great needs and the impact we can make is so small. Some of the necessary changes need to be made by citizens and governments of the wealthy countries, not simply by giving of our surplus, but by more radical change in our consumer oriented life styles."[37]

Transformation at the individual and community level needed to be accompanied by advocacy for transformation at the level of public policy and legislation. In the late 1960s, a Palestinian woman told Hedy Sawadsky, a Canadian MCC worker in the occupied West Bank, that "what you're doing here is fine, but it is only Band-Aid work. Why don't you go home and work for

---

[35] Carol Loeppky, "Oma Jean," *Intercom* 30, no. 9 (November-December 1986): 2.

[36] "MCC Statement on Program Assumptions, Objectives and Priorities," B.6.

[37] Quoted in Marr, *The Transforming Power of a Century*, 240.

peace and get at the root causes of evil and war?"[38] From the 1960s onwards, MCC workers increasingly identified U.S. and Canadian military actions, foreign policy, and trade regimes as structures that Christians should seek to dismantle and transform through public policy advocacy. Accompanying African-American communities in New Orleans and First Nations in Canada also raised questions for MCCers not only about what dismantling racism and addressing the ongoing dispossession of Indigenous peoples would look like at the national level, but also about how to address such ongoing racism and colonial legacies within Mennonite communities in the U.S. and Canada and within MCC, questions with which MCC still wrestles.

Measuring

By the early 1990s, some MCC leaders had become restless with the strong internal emphasis on presence and accompaniment, seeking to acknowledge and sharpen MCC's role in making proactive interventions in relief, development, and peacebuilding. In 1994, MCC invited theologian and missionary Norman Kraus to reflect on MCC's work, with the end product a paper on "A Theological Basis for Intervention Ministries." Kraus recognized that a missiology of presence had taken root within MCC. "We do not like to be identified as a social 'change agent,'" Kraus observed. "We just want to be a 'presence'—to stand alongside, 'to suffer with,' 'identify with,' and 'learn from.'" Yet, Kraus continued, MCC "does not send service workers into the various parts of the world merely to be respectfully and sympathetically present, but to be *catalytic* and *dialogical* change agents."[39] Kraus did not propose that MCC abandon the language of presence, but did counsel that presence be conceptualized as a mode of proactive intervention, rather than as an end in itself.

---

[38] Quoted in Leo Driedger and Donald Kraybill, *Mennonite Peacemaking: From Quietism to Activism* (Scottdale, PA: Herald Press, 1984), 137.

[39] C. Norman Kraus, *A Theological Basis for Intervention Ministries*, MCC Occasional Paper No. 20 (Akron, PA: MCC, May 1994), 3.

Such initial rumblings about rethinking the missiology of presence surfaced around the same time that MCC began initial thinking about how to engage the emerging emphasis in the early 1990s within the international humanitarian relief and development world on results-based management, or RBM, also often referred to as outcomes-based management. United Nations agencies and government donor agencies like the Canadian International Development Agency (CIDA, now Global Affairs Canada) and USAID started using RBM as a management process for planning for results. These governmental and inter-governmental donor agencies increasingly began to expect non-governmental organizations to which they gave funds to adopt RBM as well and to use RBM tools such as the so-called "logical framework" (often shortened

Fig. 56: Elaha, pictured left, and her husband Mahedi (names changed for security), were participants in 2018 in an MCC project funded by Global Affairs Canada to connect families in Afghanistan's Central Highlands to clean water sources. (MCC photo/Paul Shetler Fast)

to "logframe") as the map for project plans, tracing the anticipated relationship between relief and development activities and desired changes (outcomes) and identifying metrics (indicators) for use in tracking and quantifying progress towards that desired change. Relief, development, and peacebuilding actors adopted RBM as a tool for learning and documenting which initiatives worked well and which did not and for then making decisions about more productive and efficient use of resources. Given the fact that MCC, along with the ecumenical Canadian Foodgrains Bank (CFGB) of which MCC was a founding member, received significant funding from the Canadian government, MCC had to determine how it would engage   Canadian   government   expectations   that   the organizations it supported would adopt RBM (fig. 56). In 1997, MCC began implementing "results based" planning in the thirteen MCC country programs to which Canadian government money was applied, determined to "glean" learnings "that would be useful in all overseas MCC programs."[40] In 2004, MCC's   International   Program   Department   piloted   a standardized outcomes-based project planning, monitoring, and evaluation (PME) system in several countries, rolling it out to all country programs the following year. By 2012, MCC had developed a standardized project PME system for its work in Canada, the United States, and around the world.[41]

Could this new emphasis on measurement and results-based planning   be   squared   with   the   missiology   of   presence, accompaniment, and solidarity that had taken root and grown within MCC from the seventies into the nineties? Some in MCC saw deep tension. For some MCC program leaders, outcomes-based management represented a distinct shift away from the missiology of presence. At an MCC Binational board meeting I attended in 2001, former MCC Africa Area Director Eric Olfert, when sharing with the board about the impact of MCC program in Africa, pointed the board back to the importance of presence, connection, and relationships, offering that MCC's impact could be measured by how many cups of tea MCC workers drank with community members (fig. 57).[42] Some board members, however, wanted reporting on other types of metrics, such as increased crop production for small-landholding farmers, or decreased drop-out rates of girls in MCC-supported schools, or increased

[40] 1997 Program Planning Summary, Overseas Program Office, Objective 5b, MCC Executive Committee Meeting. #513. December 13 and 14, 1996, MCC U.S. archives, Akron, Pennsylvania.

[41] I reflected on the missiological questions raised by the adoption of results-based management for MCC's program work in "A Missiological Shift? Reflections on the Introduction of Results-Based Management within Mennonite Central Committee," *Mission Focus: Annual Review* 14 (2006): 27-41.

[42] Personal notes from meeting.

diet diversity for food insecure families. MCC, like other non-profits, also found that its supporters increasingly wanted more information about the difference, including the measurable difference, MCC programs were making in people's lives.

Fig. 57: Members of the MCC Nepal team after a meal at the MCC office in Kathmandu in 2015 with visitors from the Brethren in Community Welfare Society (BICWS). From left, Martha Kimmel, Luke Reesor-Keller, Shemlal Hembrom (BICWS director and General Secretary of Brethren in Christ churches in Nepal), Hanna Soren (BICWS), Juliana Yonzon, Durga Sunchiuri, Leah Reesor-Keller, and Kriz Cruzado. (MCC photo/Derek Lee)

Can missiologies of presence, accompaniment, connection, and solidarity be squared with the mandate to plan for, monitor, and evaluate progress towards desired outcomes? As director of MCC's planning and learning department, I not surprisingly believe that outcomes-based planning can be compatible with the missiological call to accompany and be in solidarity with marginalized communities. Certainly, strong critiques of outcomes-based planning have been advanced over the past several years. Historian Jerry Z. Muller, spurred by his consternation with what he calls "metric fixation" in academia, observes in his recent study, *The Tyranny of Metrics*, that obsession with metrics by charitable organizations can promote a "short-termism" mentality, an impatience, for example, to wait for development and peacebuilding efforts to bear fruit, and a skittishness to try innovative approaches.[43]   Meanwhile,

---

[43] Jerry Z. Muller, *The Tyranny of Metrics* (Princeton, NJ: Princeton University Press, 2018), 23, 154-155.

anthropologist Sally Engle Merry, in her book, *The Seductions of Quantification*, highlights how social location and power shape the selection of indicators, how attempts to measure impact across multiple projects and diverse contexts lead to decontextualized and homogenized data that do not represent the full richness of individual peacebuilding initiatives, and how a fixation on measurement can bewitch individuals and institutions into thinking that only that which can be measured matters.[44] Neither Muller nor Merry is dogmatically opposed to all forms of measurement. Rather, both stress that meaningful metrics are context-specific and are developed with the active participation of people to whom the metrics pertain.

Muller and Merry both rightly highlight that regimes of planning and measurement involve the exercise of power. For humanitarian agencies such as MCC, implementing an outcomes-based planning system means asking questions about what type of power is held and exercised by whom. Who is involved in identifying desired changes for a community? Who determines what will count as positive change? Who is listened to? Who is ignored or silenced? Are project metrics identified by aid agency staff? by donors? by community members? How do Christian relief, development, and peacebuilding agencies like MCC prioritize different types of accountability: to governing boards? to donors? to the churches and community-based organizations with which they partner? to the project participants who hope to benefit from MCC-supported initiatives? Are monitoring and evaluation simply forms of control—or are they exercises in learning that are open to failure and to radical adjustment? How does an agency like MCC share power with partners, let alone, in Tim Lind's words, abdicate executive authority, when government authorities like the Canada Revenue Agency expect MCC as a non-profit to maintain direction and control over money and other resources it gives to partners?

No simple, definitive answers to such questions are available: these questions identify tensions that MCC manages and

---

[44] Sally Engle Merry,*The Seductions of Quantification: Measuring Human Rights, Gender Violence, and Sex Trafficking* (Chicago: University of Chicago Press, 2016), 19-20, 216-217.

negotiates as it seeks to maintain and build on the strengths of missiologies of presence and accompaniment while also working with partners to measure and track progress towards desired change. That said, some common themes emerge in how MCC talks about power and outcomes-based approaches to change. In May 2018, in response to internal questions about what constituted MCC's theory of change, MCC program directors responded that "lasting change . . . requires long-term commitment and happens when all members of a community connect across lines of difference to actively participate in shaping and implementing visions for just social, environmental, and economic structures."[45] MCC, this statement underscored, accompanies partners and communities for the long term, a commitment that helps guard against the short-termism mentality that Muller highlights as representative of metric fixation. Furthermore, visions for change, and plans to work towards that change, must emerge from and be owned by communities themselves if that change will be sustainable. Monitoring and evaluation, meanwhile, should not be exercises in policing to ensure that MCC-supported initiatives have unfolded according to a predetermined plan, but should instead be opportunities for learning. Finally, while MCC staff are undeniably accountable to boards and donors, they are ultimately accountable to the Christ whom they encounter in the hungry, the thirsty, and the stranger in communities marginalized by oppressive economic, social, and political structures.

Over the course of nearly a century, in scores of countries around the world and amidst famine, war, disasters, revolution, military occupation, and entrenched poverty, MCC has discerned what it means to serve in the name of Christ, forged inter-Anabaptist, ecumenical, and interfaith connections that have opened new perspectives on who belongs to the household of faith, and struggled with acknowledging its power and with how to use that power. This history has included failures, surprises, and successes, moments of courageous faithfulness

---

[45] "MCC's Operating Principles and Essential Elements of Change," May 2018, MCC U.S. archives, Akron, Pennsylvania.

and events that call for lament and repentance. An institution's centennial is rightly a time of celebration. Part of MCC's one hundred years to be celebrated is a legacy of enduring self-critique. For MCC, its centennial should not only be a time a celebration, but a time for rededicating itself to ongoing grappling with what serving in the name of Christ means and what it calls Anabaptist churches in Canada and the U.S. to undertake. On the occasion of MCC's twenty-fifth anniversary in 1945, MCC leader P.C. Hiebert urged Mennonites not to mark the anniversary as a time for self-congratulation, but rather by renewed attempts at faithful service. Hiebert's appeal from 75 years ago remains relevant to today as MCC embarks on its second century:

> The encouragement derived from the past should give us no feelings of elation. Might the past rather serve as a divine precedent urging us to repeat increasingly the service then rendered. How could we better honor God at this twenty-fifth mile-stone than by rededicating ourselves to the continuation and completion of our present relief undertakings. In all of our efforts may we give a clear witness for Christ and strive 'for the faith once delivered to the saints.' With gratefulness for the past, redoubled zeal in fulfilling our present mission, and trust in God for the future let us humbly yet joyfully continue in the work now but well begun.[46]

---

[46] *Twenty-Five Years 1920-1945* (Akron, PA: Mennonite Central Committee, 1945), 3.

Index

Advocacy, 19, 23, 39, 117-118
Alternative service, 3, 27, 35, 90
American Relief Administration, 76
Anti-racism, 39, 92, 118
Apartheid, 115
Bangladesh, 95-96, 99
Bartel, Barry, 107
Beachy, Bertha, 61
Beechy, Atlee, 60, 115
Bender, Harold S., 100
Berend, W.M., 81-82
Beyeler, Robert, 48-49, 56
Bolivia, 59, 63-64, 93
Braun, Abram, 80
Brubacher, Ray, 97-98
Byler, Edna Ruth, 5, 19
Byler, J.N., 80-81, 83
Canadian Foodgrains Bank
    (CFGB), 5-6, 120
Canadian Mennonite Board of
    Colonization, 32
Chad, 31, 105
China, 83-84
Church of the Brethren, 56, 88,
    92n41
Civilian Public Service (CPS), 3, 46-
    47, 49, 53, 90-91
Classen, Susan, 8, 115
Climate change/climate crisis, xvi
Cold War, 28n15, 53, 94-95
Colonialism also colonial, post-
    colonial, colonial legacies xiii-
    xv, 30-42, 59-60, 95, 101-102,
    104, 118
Communism, 53-54
Congo, Democratic Republic of, 8,
    11, 17-18, 31, 36-37, 67-68, 88,
    93, 108
Connecting peoples, 108-118
Conscientious objection, 28, 46
Core Humanitarian Standard, 71
Council of Relief Agencies
    Licensed for Operation in
    Germany (CRALOG), 78
COVID-19, xvi, 64
Creation care, 21
Damascus Road program, 39
Deckert, Bennie, 90

Development Monographs (MCC
    publications), 103-107
Dick, Judith, 62
Driedger, Anne, 51-52
Dunant, Henry, 69-70
Dyck, Peter, 7, 47, 81-83
Eastern Mennonite Board of
    Missions and Charities, 6
Ecumenical partnerships, 10-11, 18,
    23, 69, 88-96, 109, 120, 123
Egypt, 11, 95
El Salvador, 8, 11, 28, 96, 115
Epp, Anthony, 36-37
Epp, Hans, 34
Epp-Tiessen, Esther, 15n2, 32
Ewert, Merrill, 105-106, 108
Fair trade, 5, 19
Fast, Henry, 89
Finnish Red Cross, 9
Fountain, Philip, 16
Freire, Paulo, 104-105, 107
Fretz, J. Winfield, 35-36, 75
Friedan, Betty, 51
Glaubensgenossen, 66-67
Goossen, Rachel Waltner, 1, 15n2
Graber, Abraham, 46
Greece, 50-51, 54
Guatemala, 8
Gulfport, Mississippi, 38, 61, 67
Haiti, 26, 107, 117
Händiges, Emil, 80
Harding, Vincent and Rosemarie,
    39-40
Hein, Marvin, 46-47
Heisey, Nancy, 103-105, 108
Herr, Judy Zimmerman, 61, 115
Herr, Robert, 115
Hershberger, Guy F., 75n12, 100
Hiebert, P.C., 73-74, 76-77, 124
HIV/AIDS response, 92
Honduras, 25, 93-94, 112
Hoover, Herbert, 76
Hostetter, C.N., 57, 77
Household of faith, xv, 66-69, 72-
    75, 77-88, 95, 123
Humanitarianism, xiv-xv, 42, 68-
    72, 81, 86-88, 95-97
Hunsberger, Gord and Tillie, 117

Illich, Ivan, 104
Indigenous, 14, 31-36, 39, 41, 114, 118
Indigenous Neighbours/Native Concerns program (MCC Canada), 39n29
International Committee of the Red Cross (also International Red Cross and Red Crescent Movement), 69-70
International Volunteer Exchange Program (IVEP), xiii, 63-64, 112
Interreligious partnerships, 10-11, 95
Janzen Longacre, Doris, 20-22
Jordan, 11, 95
Juhnke, James, 55-56
Lehman, M.C., 72
Kanagy, Karen, 63
Kauffman, Roy, 47-48
Kaufman, E.G., 100
Klassen, C.F., 77
Klassen Hamm, Eileen 40-41
Korea, Democratic People's Republic of (North Korea), 1, 19, 44
Korea, Republic of (South Korea), 50, 85, 93
Kratz, Clayton, 44-45
Kraus, C. Norman 118
Kreider, Robert, 15n2, 57-58, 78-81, 98
Kurtz, Hilda, 63
Kuyf, Wilhelmina, 83-84
Land acknowledgment, 14
Landscapes, imagined, xiii, xv, 14-32, 42, 65, 97
Laos (Lao People's Democratic Republic), 11, 95
Lapp, John A., 108
Lapp, Omar, 53
Lesotho, 106
Lind, Tim, 61-62, 103-104, 106-108, 122
Loeppky, Carol, 116-117
Lohrentz, Ken, 36
Malkki, Liisa, 9
Marr, Lucille, 15n2, 50

Martens, Harry, 44, 53, 54, 57, 58
Martin, Earl, 30, 115
Martin, Lois, 50
Material resources centers, xiii, 25-26
Mathies, Ronald, 4, 27, 57-58
Meat canning, xiii, 1, 4, 10, 13, 25-26, 43-44, 81
Mennonite Central Committee (MCC)
    A Commitment to Christ's Way of Peace (1994), 86, 111
    as ecumenical driver, xviin2, 69, 88-96
    as incubator, 4-6
    as inter-Anabaptist/inter-Mennonite, xiii-xv, 26-27, 89-90, 93-95, 113
    as ministry of reconciliation, 2-3, 8-9, 12-13
    as rhizome-like network, 24
    foundation of, 10
    histories of, 15n2
    in Akron, Pennsylvania, 24
    logos of, 110-111
    missiology of, xiv-xvi, 2, 97-100, 107-108, 111, 118-120
    organizational whiteness of, 39n30, 61
    Ottawa office, 20n7
    Principles that Guide Our Mission (1999), 109-110
    Washington, D.C. office, 19-20, 93
Mennonite Conciliation Service, 29, 92-93n42
Mennonite Disaster Service (MDS), 4-5
Mennonite World Conference (MWC), xiii, 27, 63, 94, 112
Mental health work, 4-5, 49, 52, 67, 91
Merry, Sally Engle, 122
Miller, Orie O., 24, 72-74
Missio Dei, 103
Modernization theory, 32, 103-104, 108
More-with-Less Cookbook, 20-22, 117
Muller, Jerry Z., 121-123

Mutual transformation. *See* Service: as mutual transformation
Nepal, 93, 113, 121
New Orleans, 61, 118
Nicaragua, 28, 87, 115
Nigeria, 24, 26, 36, 88
Nonresistance, 27, 44-45, 55, 74, 90
Olfert, Eric, 120
Outcomes-based management. *See* Results-based management
Palestine-Israel, 11, 21-23, 29, 30
Paraguay, 4, 26, 32-35, 66
Pax, xiii, 3, 4, 10, 27, 34-35, 44, 47-59, 90
Peace Section/Peace Office, 58, 90-93
Peace theology, 27, 90-92, 95
Peachey, Urbane, 58-59
Penashue, Elizabeth, 41
Presence. *See* Service: as presence
Puidoux Conferences, 92n41
Quakers, 11, 68, 92n41, 95
Racism, xiv-xv, 39, 61, 92, 118
Refugees, relief work with and resettlement of, 12, 23n10, 29-30, 32-33, 46, 64, 66, 79, 92
Relief sales, xiv, 4, 10, 18-19, 26
Results-based management, 100, 119-120
Revolution, 8, 28-29, 95, 115, 123
Russia, xiii, xvi, 1, 32, 43-45, 66-67, 73-77, 93
Sawadsky, Hedy, 117
Schlabach, Gerald, 115
Schlabach, Lydia, 50, 85
SELFHELP Crafts, 5, 19
Service,
    as constructed and contested, xv, 15-17
    as distinct from evangelism, 6, 57
    as education or transformative education, 57-58
    as eschatological hope made visible, 7
    as form of patriotism, 53-55
    as going the second mile, 2-3, 20, 46, 48
    as mutual transformation, 38, 109-111
    as presence, xvi 22, 28, 31, 58, 61, 62, 97, 99, 100-102, 106-108, 111, 116-121, 123
    as racialized, 18, 30-33, 38, 60-61
    as relief, 43-44
    as solidarity, 28, 100, 114-116, 120-121
    as translated, 16
    as unidirectional, xv, 38, 57, 60, 113,
Serving and Learning Together (SALT), 62, 64
Serving with Appalachian Peoples/Sharing with Appalachian Peoples (SWAP), 62, 116
Sider, Rich, 87
Simple living, 21
Smith, C. Henry, 100
Snyder, Jean, 62
Snyder, William, 78, 83-85, 94, 101, 115
Solidarity. *See* Service: as solidarity
Solferino, Battle of, 69
South Africa, 30, 95, 115
Soviet Union, 32, 80n23
Sphere Standards, 70-71
Stoesz, Edgar, 101, 103-105, 108
Swalm, E.J., 58, 85
Swartzendruber, Dorothy, 47
Syria, xvi, 1, 11-13, 28, 44, 88
Teachers Abroad Program (TAP), xiii, 4, 17-18, 36-37, 51-52
Ten Thousand Villages, 5, 19
Thrift shops, xiv, 10, 25-26
Toews, Reg, 86, 98-99, 108
Trans-Chaco Highway, 34-35
Ukraine, 11, 40, 78, 95
Unruh, John, 15n2, 76, 89, 93
Vietnam, 28, 30, 95
Voluntary Service (VS), 38, 51, 54, 56
Warkentin, Tina, 51
Wiebe, Dwight, 54
World Council of Churches, 92n41
World War I, xvi, 44, 70

World War II, xiii, 3-5, 27-28, 35,
    44-46, 53, 66, 69, 83, 89, 93, 95
Yoder-Bontrager, Daryl, 113-114
Young Anabaptist Mennonite
    Exchange Network (YAMEN)
    63-65, 112
Young Chippewayan, 40-41
Zaire. *See* Congo, Democratic
    Republic of
Zimbabwe, 26, 30, 93
Zook Barge, Elaine, 113-114